1 of 160: Foundations of My Freshman Year

A Memoir by Amman F. Asfaw

1 of 160: Foundations of My Freshman Year

Published in 2022 by Gen Z(eal) Publications

www.amman.win — amman.win@gmail.com

Front cover logo: Tunmi Da Silva, 2016
Back cover photo: Nicholas Kovac, 2020
Cover and text design: Amman Fasil Asfaw, 2022
Editor: Daria Majlessi

First printing: November 2022
ISBN-13: 979-8-9865629-0-2

For my grandmas, Adey Hiwot & Mama Amlesu.

Contents

Tables

Figures

Whoever is in need of advice
undoubtedly will find it.

Abba Shenouda III,
The Life of Repentance and Purity (1990)

1

Preface: 160 of 22,000

Fall 2022

The first prize I won in college was a black t-shirt with loud, white, graffiti-like font saying, "1 of 160," on the front and "Unapologetically Black" on the back. I earned it after winning a water balloon toss competition at a Black Student Union (BSU) cookout in October 2016—my first month of freshman year.

When I asked what "1 of 160" was referring to, I was told of the 21,306 students at our university, approximately 152 students identified as African-American [1]. 152 divided by 21,306 equals 0.71%. The turnout at the barbecue was so low they gave me two shirts.

I kept one shirt for my wardrobe, which I still have to this day. The other shirt I cut up and pinned as a bedside wall decoration for all five years of college.

Five years later, by the time I graduated and took down the 1 of 160 wall decor to move out, not much changed statistically. Out of the 22,022 students at our university, approximately 159 students identified as African-American [2]. 159 divided by 22,022 equals 0.72%.

For perspective, if white students at my university had a similar shirt it would say, "1 of 11,716" [2]... probably in Times New Roman font. I attended the whitest (53.2%) public university in California [3].

For context, the 2021 U.S. Census says 35.2% of California's population is white (not Hispanic or Latino) while 6.5% of California's population is Black or African-American [4].

—

I don't know what this series of books will culminate to, but I can assure you it will be authentic, empowering, and insightful. You are on this journey with me, and along the way I will pull from my trove of collegiate experiences. Have faith and trust that by the end of this book series, you will be better prepared to efficiently and ethically finesse any institutionalized system of higher learning by creating a solid personal foundation.

Underrepresented and first-generation students at predominantly white institutions (PWI) need to digest an honest, unabridged collegiate narrative from a student mentor they can relate to—especially Black students—so they can matriculate then graduate in today's ever competitive educated society. Although there are mentor-mentee programs at every school, not everyone falls into an ideal mentor-mentee pairing, and many students are not comfortable enough to seek mentorship programs in the first place.

Maybe you haven't found a helpful resource to guide you through your PWI. Or maybe you're about to attend a PWI and want to be better prepared for it. Or perhaps you're a loving parent trying to better understand what your child is going through at their PWI. Either way, I'm confident anyone connected in any shape, way, or form to a PWI can benefit from this book. My mission with this autoethnographical publication is to effectively share, with you, how I successfully navigated a predominantly white institution as a Black man.

I'm not worried about institutional pushback. This is for you, the student. I just tell it like it is. Any stories I share are 100% true. Forgive me in advance because I'm walking the tightrope of attempting to appropriately discuss an often inappropriate era of life.

I don't want to scare you away from higher education. Instead, I hope my stories serve as a wake up call or eye-opener to naive or ignorant folks who may not have believed in or considered discriminatory experiences for underrepresented or first-generation students. I'm not saying everyone will go through a similar experience, because mine is quite specific. I am saying, however, that you need to be aware of the institutional nuances of your PWI, so that you and your college can mutually capitalize on each other—rather than the school solely capitalizing on you.

Recognize that you are a unicorn on campus. A unicorn is rare, desirable, and unique—but very difficult to find. People value unicorns highly. Value yourself in the same regard.

Ethnic Origin	Undergraduate		Post-Baccalaureate		Graduate		Total	
Hispanic/Latino	3,278	16.0%	36	19.7%	93	13.3%	3,407	16.0%
African American	147	0.7%	0	0.0%	5	0.7%	152	0.7%
Native American	29	0.1%	1	0.5%	1	0.1%	31	0.1%
Hawaiian/Pacific Isl	29	0.1%	0	0.0%	2	0.3%	31	0.1%
Asian American	2,565	12.6%	4	2.2%	63	9.0%	2,632	12.4%
Multi-Racial	1,458	7.1%	14	7.7%	35	5.0%	1,507	7.1%
White	11,517	56.4%	106	57.9%	403	57.8%	12,026	56.4%
Non-Resident Alien	450	2.2%	6	3.3%	33	4.7%	489	2.3%
Unknown/Other	953	4.7%	16	8.7%	62	8.9%	1,031	4.8%
Total Students	**20,426**		**183**		**697**		**21,306**	

Figure 1.1: Student ethnicity demographics during my first year at Cal Poly [1]. Published by Cal Poly's Office of Institutional Research, Fall 2016. Note: Ethnic origin is self-reported.

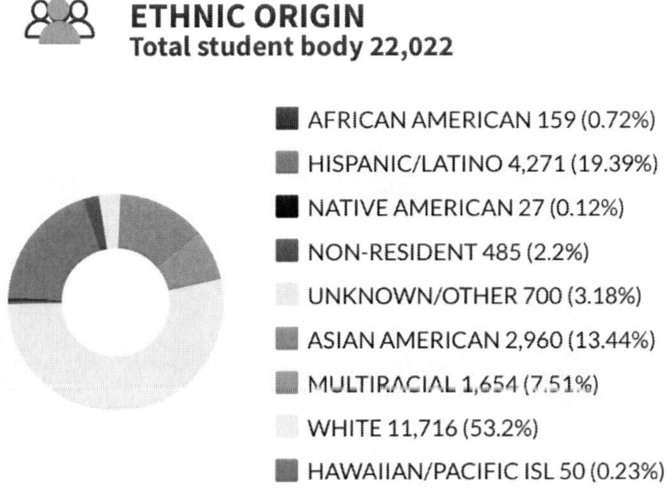

Figure 1.2: Student ethnicity demographics during my last year at Cal Poly [2]. Published by Cal Poly's Office of Institutional Research, Fall 2021. Note: Ethnic origin is self-reported.

My words do not intend to come from a place of superiority; rather, they come from a place of dedication, good intention, and love for my community. I genuinely want to see everyone succeed (on their terms, of course), because if I can help a person accomplish their goals, then I am victorious as well.

Each chapter begins with a relevant quote that resonates with me and the chapter's topic. Since high school, I've kept a running list of lyrics, quotes, and excerpts on my phone. I included these quotes to show I look up to role models who inspire and teach me various life lessons. Please don't think I came up with all this "wisdom" on my own. Everything I write in this book is a result of me learning from others or my failures. Now it's my turn to share the knowledge with you.

There is much to spend your time and energy on in college: volunteering, leadership roles, activism, jobs, study abroad, fitness, politics, art, advocacy, relationships, and the list goes on.

Before you focus on these though, I challenge you to invest your time and energy on creating a solid personal foundation of faith, mentality, and community. We are a generation that has sadly lost touch with ourselves and humanity, in part because we lack firm personal foundations.

Faith prevents wandering. Mentality prevents quitting. Community promotes wellness.

This book contains the true stories of how at the age of 18 I began to discover and build a personal foundation of faith, mentality, and community which became the launchpad for all my future successes.

Your collegiate life story will surely be different, but you can definitely learn from mine... or at least be entertained.

Welcome to college and good luck, my friend :)

Part I

ORIENTATION

I used to pray for times like this, to rhyme like this.
So I had to grind like that, to shine like this.

Meek Mill, "Intro" (2012)

2

Corny Icebreakers

Spring Quarter, 2019

It's the spring quarter of my junior year studying electrical engineering at Cal Poly, and I second guess myself: "Can I really write and publish a book? All while pursuing an engineering degree?" I head to my room to do a quick Google search on what I specifically want to write about, with the hopes that I'll find an already published book on the topic, so I can scrap my idea and move on with my evening.

I find nothing.

I shake my head with a mix of relief and fear. Relief, because my creativity produced what seems like a truly original idea—not the easiest task for an engineer—and fear, because I would be the first one to author such a perspective[1]. Anxious,

[1]Years later I discovered "The Only Black Student" by Lull Mengesha.

because publishing a book on anything even remotely controversial may affect my future job opportunities. Trepidation, because even if I somehow published this book, what if it flops; becoming irrelevant and a waste of my time? Just some good ol' self-doubt—something every college student deals with.

After fighting my inner self doubt by weighing the pros and cons, I determine this is a potential opportunity for me to pounce on. Awesome. I sleep on it for a night or two then begin brainstorming and listing chapter titles in my phone. I even create a Word doc building the template for my well-intentioned concept. Wow, this is a great start. Now let me find some legitimate excuses *not* to undertake this project. Ah yes, the classic collegiate charade of graciously avoiding responsibility by way of excuse.

But that's exactly what I do. In fact, I do this for over two years since I'm swamped with school work, volunteering, protesting, and social life. For two years, I leave the idea to simmer on the back burner of my mind, occasionally adding to it, but mostly succumbing to the various barriers my mind manufactures.

Summer 2021

It's now 2021. I work and live in a new city (Oakland) because I recently graduated from college. If I want to fulfill this literary dream, I can't wait any longer. This is it. This is the perfect time.

I pray for the strength to see it through, God willing. I set mini goals so this dream is more manageable. I create a daily writing plan that works with my full-time job schedule. I find a better software program for writing. I tell others of this aspiration as a way of manifestation. Then, I write, and I write, and I write some more. It's exhausting.

If you're reading this, it's *not* too late. It's not too late for you to reach for the stars and achieve your most ambitious ideas. I can attest as this book is my testament.

You'll learn more about me as you read, but let's start with the ever-lame but classic college activity: the icebreaker. Get used to these, as they'll be the forgettable and uncomfortable beginnings to some of your best relationships in college. So here's my generic icebreaker (if we haven't broken it already): My name is Amman Fasil Asfaw. I'm a 24-year-old recent graduate of Cal Poly where I completed my bachelor's and master's degrees in electrical engineering. My parents were born in different parts of Ethiopia and immigrated to America in the 1990s, so I'm a first-generation Ethiopian-American born in California. I was pretty involved on campus. I participated in the National Society of Black Engineers (NSBE), Black Student Union (BSU), and Sigma Nu Fraternity. Fun facts: I studied abroad for a quarter in San Sebastián-Donostia, Spain, my favorite pastime is basketball, and my first name means "peace" in Tigrinya and Amharic.

If you think this is all kind of lame, cheesy, or not worth it, then feel free to stop reading and carry on with your day. BUT JUST KNOW, this is unfortunately how most relationships and involvements on college campuses start. Generic, boring, and uncomfortable. But if you stick with it, it will pay off. Trust me. The number of students I've witnessed not come back to a person or group because their initial interactions were awkward is truly a shame. Sometimes I just want to yell, "it's supposed to be awkward, embrace it!" but I don't, because maybe they're just not ready yet—which is okay.

Disclaimer: Academically, I believe Cal Poly is an overall phenomenal school. The classes are challenging, the hiring rate for graduates is exceptional because we're near Silicon Valley, and the cost of attendance is as cheap as it gets in America's overpriced, for-profit education system. I have no regrets at all in choosing Cal Poly—I'm actually extremely glad I ended up there and am super grateful to have had the opportunity to receive such high quality education. With that said, Cal Poly—just like any other school—has its own areas for improvement; specifically with diversity, equity, and inclusivity.

It is not a carol of joy or glee,
But a prayer that he sends from his heart's deep core,
But a plea, that upward to Heaven he flings—
I know why the caged bird sings!

Paul Laurence Dunbar, "Sympathy" (1899)

3

Caged Bird Sings

Fall Quarter, 2018

For context, 2018 was quite an unsettling and problematic year for Cal Poly. To briefly summarize, on April 7th, 2018, an on-campus fraternity, Lambda Chi Alpha, was exposed for having a gangster-themed brotherhood event where several students dressed as "Mexican cholos" and one student committed blackface by literally painting every square inch of his neck and face pitch black [5]. Just Google "Cal Poly blackface" and you'll see. The incident received international media attention, there were protests on campus, and the rest of our school year was flooded with exhausting but necessary conversations regarding diversity and inclusion.

In fact, dialogue continued into the next academic school year—my junior year. In November 2018, Cal Poly Magazine, which is a part of Cal Poly's University Marketing department, reached out to me via email asking if I'd be interested in "sharing my perspective on the last year" in 450 words or less for their "Lessons Learned in 2018" feature within their triannual publication. Typically, I would respectfully pass on an opportunity like this because the institution has much more to gain from this than I do. However, since I was individually emailed about it not once, not twice, but three separate times by two different Cal Poly Magazine employees—one being the magazine's editor—I figured I'd write a submission.

To be fair, in their eyes, my student perspective at the time was a hot commodity . In May 2018, my school's newspaper, Mustang News, wrote an article on how my fraternity elected me to become the first ever diversity chair within Cal Poly's Greek life [6]. Weeks after, all fraternities and sororities within the Interfraternity Council (IFC) and The Panhellenic Association (PHA) were required to create and elect a diversity chair. So in a way, I felt it was my duty to provide my perspective—even though it was nearing the end of my quarter and I needed to focus on my final exams. I decided to be as honest as possible while still sticking to the prompt: What lessons did you learn in 2018? I'll let my original submission speak for itself.

3.1 *Lessons Learned* (Essay)

> "What lessons did I learn in 2018? Well, for an African-American, Cal Poly can feel like four years of *Get Out* (the movie). You know the scene where Chris meets his girlfriend's extended family for the first time?... yeah, kind of like that.
>
> All jokes aside though, African-Americans at predominantly white institutions (PWI's) shouldn't

feel that way. So, how do we actively change that? GRASSROOTS.

I'm no expert in this topic (and you probably aren't either), but I can confidently speak on my unique experiences as a black male at Cal Poly. Currently, I'm Vice President of Cal Poly's National Society of Black Engineers (NSBE), *and* Diversity Director of Cal Poly's Sigma Nu Fraternity, which is predominantly white. So, it's fair to say I witness "both sides" of Cal Poly.

At Cal Poly, grassroots efforts are the most realistic way to ultimately change this school's reputation as the whitest public university in California—and that's not an exaggeration... Google it. How do you think any social/political movements of modern history began? The answer *must* be grassroots movements—because I know damn well it ain't being started by figureheads in positions of institutional power and/or privilege.

I've found my experiences with grassroots efforts in my fraternity this past year to be surprisingly successful. To me, grassroots efforts come in two forms: CONVERSATION and ACTION. Each are effective, but both are necessary to make a positive change. Face-to-face conversation is naturally where it starts. But here's the key: the less people in the discussion, the more impactful the conversation will be. Also, the more candid and casual it is—hence a "conversation"—the more honest the discussion will be. (Now imagine how effective those ridiculously large diversity talks are).

Action is the most challenging component of a grassroots movement in Cal Poly's Greek life. But here's

> the key: the action should be done with the intent to go unpublicized by media. If any action is executed with the premise it will be publicized, then the ultimate goal of said action is lost in the "e-clout." Organizations/institutions don't need a news story or publicity stunt to prove or disprove their inclusivity... if you know, you know.
>
> I'm a big metaphor guy, so let me analogize. There's genuinely good people on "both sides" of Cal Poly. But often, people don't see or have the avenue to reach out to their peers on the "other side." So, there must be people who are conscious enough to strategically build a path to bridge the gap. Once the bridge is built, you'd be genuinely surprised at how many people meet halfway on the bridge, or better yet, go to the "other side" to really make a positive difference.

What do you think? It's not that controversial, right? I kept it one hundred and answered the prompt pretty well, in my opinion. I specifically remember the night I wrote the submission. I decided to sacrifice over three hours of my Saturday night, about three weeks before my final exams, to convert my raw and complicated feelings into digestible words.

Wouldn't it be a shame if Cal Poly Magazine—part of an institution—tried to ask me to "do a bit of an edit" to my first paragraph because it might be "easy to misinterpret or misunderstand, especially for people who haven't seen" the movie? Well, that's exactly what happened. They wanted to soften and ultimately censor my real perspective to cater to their readers, thus better positioning Cal Poly to receive more money from donors. But hey, I'm a reasonable guy; and maybe there was room for improvement with my wording. So two weeks before my final exams, I sent Cal Poly Magazine an annotated version of my submission commenting on what I was "potentially willing to consider changing". But I stressed I did not want the "message of my submission" to be lost.

Now, wouldn't it be ironically audacious for the institutionalized editor to respond suggesting, "what do you think about being more direct there and specifying the actual feelings you experience?" Well, once again, that's exactly what happened. So one week before my final exams, my patient yet witty self respectfully provided the magazine editor with a second edit of my intro, making it painstakingly clear my Get Out reference was a hyperbole—a creative figure of speech. Here's the second edit of the intro I sent to the editor (the bolded words were new to the edit):

> What lessons did I learn in 2018? Well, for an African-American, Cal Poly ***can*** **feel** like four years of the movie, Get Out—**it's a hyperbole, relax.** You know the scene where Chris meets his girlfriend's extended family for the first time?... **yeah, it's like that sometimes.**

Although I wasn't too stoked on this edit, I felt it still would have been a win for Black students at PWIs. But I made it clear to them I didn't want my submission published without the Get Out reference. The editor responded wisely, requesting to set up a phone call since it was getting wordy over email. I totally agreed. So I took it a step further and requested to meet in person so they couldn't mask their institutionalization behind a telephone. But of course, since I was in the middle of my always stressful final exam week, we set the in-person meeting for the day after my last exam—the first day of my winter break.

I showed up to the Cal Poly University Marketing office on campus and was a bit surprised meeting the editor. He was a short, young man, late twenties or maybe early thirties, fashionably dressed in a grey vest, plaid dress shirt, and matching tie if I remember correctly. And on top of that his last name clearly indicated he came from Hispanic origin. I was caught off guard because I guess I was expecting an older white man based on the caucasity of his tone and timing over email... interesting.

Nonetheless, we had a civil and productive 30 minute conversation in his office. I was comfortable and he was comfortable from what I could tell. I explained in more detail the context of my submission and he claimed to completely understand where I was coming from. He elaborated how it was his "boss" who he was afraid wouldn't approve of my submission, specifically the intro. But he assured me he was confident and optimistic the submission shouldn't have a problem being approved after hearing me out in person. So we ended on a high note and I went and enjoyed a well deserved winter break.

Until I received an email from the editor about two weeks later. As soon as I saw the email's subject title, "Opening paragraphs," I knew exactly what was coming and immediately laughed at the obviousness of my PWI's inability to swallow such a tiny pill of truth. It's like a kid that doesn't want to take their vitamins. I even wrapped the truth up in a gummy bear of humor, and they still couldn't swallow it LOL. Granted, this was Cal Poly's University Marketing department I was dealing with, so of course one of their primary objectives is to display Cal Poly in a positive light, just like any other marketing department. But that also means they're willing to accomplish said objectives at the expense of students' true perspectives and opinions. Are you starting to see the issue here?

The email regarding the "Opening paragraphs" mentioned how my message was being discussed amongst the editor's "boss and her boss" and how they were "both really hesitant about putting the university's official stamp of approval on comparing Cal Poly to such a negative situation, no matter how true it may be to people's experience." He might as well have called it the university's official stamp of systemic oppression. I didn't know one accurate movie comparison and reference could cause such a ruckus. Since I wasn't budging on writing exactly what they wanted, the editor desperately decided to take "a crack at adding in" the context of the intro I described at our in-person meeting, in hopes of garnering approval from the bosses. Why does this sound like some kiss-the-ring type of loyalty from The Godfather...? Damn, another movie comparison LOL.

Fortunately, the editor was self-aware of his bold attempt prefacing it with "I know you didn't want to change the intro much, but please take a look at what I've added below and let me know if you're ok with this. I hope it hasn't taken anything away from your meaning. If you don't think this is ok, I totally understand, but I'm not sure she'll let me publish without something like this." Here was his attempt (the bolded words were his new additions):

> "**At a meeting of the Cal Poly chapter of the National Society of Black Engineers (NSBE) this year, an alumnus guest speaker told us how he had felt about his experience as an African-American student at Cal Poly, and I'll never forget his metaphor. 'For us,** Cal Poly can feel like four years of the movie Get Out.'
>
> **Everyone in the room started laughing, because we all completely understood the feelings of alienation and intimidation he was talking about.** All jokes aside though..."

Although the added historical context of where I got the movie comparison from (shoutout to Lacy Billingsly III) was accurate, the extra fluff downplayed and masked the hook in my opinion. And I'm not bringing all this up to debate whether my version was more effective than his edited version. That's not the point. The point here is the principle of the editor—again, part of an institution—providing me with the words that I should claim as my own. That is problematic.

I responded respectfully deciding not to edit my piece any further for the sake of my time, academics, mental health, and overall well-being. If they wanted to use the version agreed upon in person, then they were welcome. Ultimately, the editor genuinely apologized via email and the magazine did not publish my piece—an outcome I was at peace with.

Included in my response was the reasoning behind why I did not want to edit any further and the reason I felt the entire situation was problematic. To begin, reworking the intro for "approval" was actually causing me to stress more than it should have. Perhaps because it made me feel like I was succumbing to being a corporate or political pawn, or perhaps because I found it ironic I was being censored—even slightly—in 2019, in the land of the free(dom of speech).

I specifically remember a couple nights where I attempted editing the hook, and I felt the opposite of Black excellence. I felt so conflicted knowing I could have a platform to speak my truth—but not an authentic truth. In those moments, I felt weak and depressed, not knowing exactly how to comprehend what was happening. I was in need of assurance, positivity, and restoration. For me, I get this through music—specifically the genre sometimes called conscious rap.

One of my creative projects as Diversity Director for my fraternity was creating a three hour music playlist titled, "Food 4 Thought," hoping it would allow my predominantly white brothers to critically think and interpret each song's unique message. I described the playlist as "Black, conscious, uncensored hip hop and another form of cultural education" [7].

After a few of the playlist's songs on shuffle, J. Cole's track, *Caged Bird (feat. Omen)*, came on. I started to cry. I put the song on repeat, sat at my desk in my room, and bobbed my head to the oh-so-relevant lyrics accompanied by the melancholic bass, while tears rolled down my cheeks. That song was what I needed. Oh, how I felt like a caged bird in that moment. It was as if they were finally going to place my "cage" front and center for everyone to hear and see my painful beauty, only for them to put my "cage" back in the basement along with the "cages" of my Black brothers and sisters. In the words of J. Cole, why won't they "let this little caged bird sing?" I didn't know where the pain was coming from. It just kind of happened, but I knew it was deep. So I seeked more inspiration.

While studying the lyrics, I learned J. Cole directly referenced the late Maya Angelou's 1969 autobiography, *I Know Why the Caged Bird Sings* [8], as well as her 1983 poem, Caged Bird [9]. The poem beautifully described my personal predicament and left me again teary eyed, but more healed. Then, diving deeper, I learned Maya Angelou selected those titles with inspiration from Paul Laurence Dunbar's 1899 poem, *Sympathy* [10]. I was again tearful after reading Dunbar's answer to the profound and metaphorical question of why the caged bird sings. Dunbar's conclusion was the solace and closure I was looking for. Maybe my piece was a plea from the heart—a prayer—disguised with humor, that I would be accepted into Heaven, thus ceasing any hardships related to my PWI.

So after all this heavy introspection, I of course shared the links to *Caged Bird*, the song and the poem, with the editor in the most elegant (yet slightly petty) way possible so he could maybe see what I was going through. I let him know I was okay with the piece not being published to the magazine's vast audience, but at the very least I hoped he and his bosses learned something new... which I was totally okay with, because that's ultimately the essence of grassroots efforts. Here was the last email I sent the editor:

> Thank you for the apology. I wasn't necessarily frustrated by your edit (or you) because I understand you're doing your job. It's just the big picture of it all that's stressful... the fact that the problem is bigger than you and me. It's deeply engrained institutionally and socially.
>
> The reason Cal Poly Marketing may feel uncomfortable approving my piece is the same reason African-Americans feel uncomfortable at Cal Poly.
>
> You make a good point in that I could be a voice for change. So, I respectfully challenge you and all of Cal Poly Marketing to wholeheartedly reconsider your mission statement, bylaws, and/or core values and see what you all—as an institution—can change (deep within) to be more inclusive now and going forward... rather than me change my genuine words.
>
> Anyway, I'd rather just lay this to rest for the sake of my time, academics, mental health, and overall well being. I hope you understand. My apologies for the long-winded email. I look forward to reading the magazine—with or without my piece—when it comes out[1]. Good luck!
>
> Best,
>
> Amman

—

[1] My piece did not make it into their final publication [11].

This incident occurred my junior year when I had my personal foundation more solidified. I did not bend to the editor nor did I lose my self-control or values in handling the situation.

First, I had faith and hope in a better future for my school when many of my peers did not. This allowed me the opportunity to present potentially meaningful solutions for my community on an official platform.

But despite my optimism, I protected my mentality by limiting my level of engagement according to my available bandwidth and ultimately knowing when to cut things off. If I would have over committed myself to their request, it likely would have come at the cost of my final exam performance and thus cumulative GPA.

And all throughout this I leaned on my community to keep me in check by consulting select people who I respected and trusted. I recall sanity checking my letter and responses with my roommate, neighbor, and peers in the Black Academic Excellence Center on campus.

I share this story before any others to show how starting in college people will try to use you for their own benefit. But with a sound personal foundation, you can deflect anything that threatens you and your people's stability. Threats to your well-being and attempts to exploit you will only get worse after college, so it's better you realize now. Granted, the exchange of services and favors is a natural part of life. But I advise you to be savvy and sociopolitically aware of your contributions because there could be times where you're doing things "for the greater good" but unknowingly sabotaging yourself or people who look like you.

Look at how institutionalized our American education systems can be. It's usually difficult to find concrete examples of institutional racism and systemic oppression because it's deeply ingrained in the fabric that holds society's systems together.

And oftentimes the disadvantages are dispersed faintly yet consistently over a long period of time, sometimes generations.

The same way flour is baked into bread, inequality is baked into our systems. If the concoction contains excess of any ingredient, you cannot salvage the baked bread. You cannot reform the bread. Nor can you dismantle the bread. The only way to correct the mistake is to bake the next batch of bread with the proper ingredients.

It all reminds me of a proverbial Tigrinya rhyme my grandma once said which loosely translates to:

> *If you add too much salt, you'll be ashamed. But if you do not add enough salt, you won't be ashamed.*

There comes a time when an unwavering will, a strong belief, and endless prayers bring great visions to realization.
Attallah Shabazz, "The Autobiography of Malcolm X" (1989)

4

Pray First

Fall 2015

It's dark out and our home is quiet when my grandma asks me in Tigrinya, "how much time is left?" Distracted, I check the clock. I respond, "uhhh 40 minutes," in my trademark mix of elementary Tigrinya and broken Amharic. She whispers, "okay good, I'm going to go pray".

My chicken legs are sore from indoor bear crawl drills during high school basketball training, but I return my focus to the desktop computer screen. I'm proofreading my essays, researching statistics, sifting through forum posts, and checking my fantasy basketball team.

In the background I hear wailing from my maternal grandma who we call Adey Hiwot (pronounced "ah-day he-what") which translates to "Mama Hiwot" in Tigrinya. Her name, Hiwot, means "life." I can't understand a word she's shouting but I know it's profound. The grief in her voice worries me so I get up from our living room's corner "office" to peak through the door and into our front porch.

Thankfully, all is good. It's just Adey Hiwot belting a daily hymn into the night to commemorate the Orthodox Easter fasting period. She does this every year for 55 straight days. She doesn't worry about what the neighbors will think. She doesn't worry about perfecting the pitch of her hymn. Palms open to the heavens, eyes closed shut, draped in a large *netsela* (scarf), she just chants and sings to God.

Adey Hiwot's life story is a mystery to me. We moved her from her countryside village in Fik'ada, Tigray, Ethiopia to our suburban apartment in Thousand Oaks[1], California when I was in 6th grade. A devout Orthodox Tewahedo Christian, she prays about five times a day and fasts from meat and dairy over half the year. She never received any formal education because in the 1940s, girls in her village weren't permitted to attend school. As a result, she is illiterate in her native tongue, Tigrinya. But boy is she sharp. Even into her late 70s, she recites the names of all 32 of her grandchildren with ease and accurately recalls the dates of decades-old historical events she lived through. In fact, we're convinced she secretly understands English from hearing us speak it in the household over the years.

She wraps up her prayer and I hustle back to the computer because I don't want her to know I was watching. My focus returns to crafting my essays for college applications. I don't have the luxury of hiring a professional to "edit" my essays like some of my friends, but I find plenty of helpful resources on the open internet.

[1]Known as *Sap'wi* ("House of the Deer") by the native Chumash peoples.

For better or for worse, I treat writing as if it is spoken word in the written form because public speaking comes natural to me. I spoke at my middle school promotion, high school graduation, and eventually one of my virtual college commencement ceremonies. Adey Hiwot shuffles back inside to begin making tea for my mom, who is known as "Mama" by many Habeshas[2].

Most nights I watch Mama hustle out the door around 10:30 PM, on her way to work the graveyard shift at the hospital. Adey Hiwot and I always wish her a good night, but sometimes the door slams before our farewells reach her ears. She's a reserved introvert who greatly enjoys her privacy, even among those closest to her.

Fortunately, Mama did receive a formal public education in Ethiopia since she was sent to live in the country's capital city at 11 years old. After high school she went to a trade school for accounting, but her certification wasn't recognized in the United States. She then repeated her accounting certification at an accredited American program, but halfway through she gave birth to me. Mama dropped her accountant ambitions and eventually settled into a lifelong career as a certified nurse assistant for Kaiser Permanente.

Hiwot plops onto our leather couch next to the computer. I think my essays are coming out okay: "My ancestors were forced to eat raw beef to avoid revealing their whereabouts during guerilla warfare." "My mom was born in a cave in order to avoid the seasonal hyena stampedes." "My grandma is now blind due to the poor ventilation of her rock-hewn kitchen back home."

Playing the immigrant card or any victim card is like a game of poker. You gotta know when to double down on it and

[2]A pan-ethnic identifier that refers to Semitic language-speaking and predominantly Orthodox Christian peoples found in the highlands of modern-day Ethiopia and Eritrea [12]

when to hold... but never fold though! Read the institution's cues. How strong is their hand? Are they sitting on a sub-one-percent Black demographic? How have they played previous hands? Conservatively or aggressively? Do they reek of white guilt?

Whatever hand you are dealt in life, I recommend playing your cards wisely and being hyper-aware of the sociopolitical sphere around you. Not only can you use these skills when applying to colleges, but also for applying to scholarships while in college. It's second nature to me now. Can you tell which of my immigrant-card claims is a bluff?[3] In five years, I earned $29,775 from 24 different essay-based scholarships... we'll talk money later.

It's now a quarter past eleven and Hiwot retires for the night. Shortly thereafter, Daddy waltzes through the front door. "Hi, Amman! You're still working?" as we kiss each other on each cheek. He goes by "Fasil", a common Ethiopian name—and a quite fitting one at that—because it sounds exactly like *facil* in Spanish, an affirmation of his easy-going personality.

Daddy was born in the modern-day capital of Ethiopia, Addis Ababa[4]. Fasil received a formal education through private schools. After high school, he dodged mandatory enlistment by pursuing his athletic ambitions as an amateur boxer sponsored and trained by the Ethiopian Navy. During his childhood, the aristocratic imperial Ethiopia was overthrown by a communist totalitarian military junta and there was little opportunity in the country. My parents lived through a genocidal state-led repression called the Ethiopian Red Terror where up to 750,000 people were killed from 1976 to 1978 [13].

It's no wonder Daddy escaped the country, seeking asylum in Nairobi, Kenya. Within a year, he lucked out and moved to

[3]Hint: There are two truths and a lie.

[4]Known as *Finfinne* ("Natural Spring") by the native Oromo peoples.

the United States, where he received his green card (permanent resident status). After unsuccessful attempts at adult schooling, Daddy eventually settled into a lifelong career in grocery stores, where he passionately manages liquor and wine to this day. Most of his life he's also worked a secondary part-time job, like shipping textbooks for the Center for Civic Education, or driving for Uber.

I'm still stuck on the damn computer, but I take a break because Daddy prepares a quick feast of his trademark late night "snack" of *tibs* (sautéed beef) with injera, an Ethiopian flatbread. My little sister ventures out of the cove of her room to dine with us. Her name is Samhal (pronounced *Semhal*) which is the Tigrinya word for a sanctified and good-smelling mint plant native to Eastern Tigray, Ethiopia (*Mentha longifolia typhoides* [14]). She is three and a half years younger than me and my only sibling.

Like me, Samhal has always attended public schools for formal education. She eventually made her way into higher education by studying biochemistry at the University of California Santa Barbara (UCSB). She will be graduating in UCSB's Class of 2023. She impresses me because she never caves into the family pressure to perform as I did. Samhal is the right-brained child and I'm the left-brained one. She's short, I'm tall. She's spontaneous, I'm calculated. I think it makes for a good family balance.

The three of us cater to our late night munchies on a single family-style tray as is customary in East Africa. Daddy and I devour our shares like we've never had meat before while Samhal eats carefully to avoid the spicy jalapeños. The meal is exactly what I need to make one more push on my essays before I go to sleep. It's midnight and Daddy heads to the shower. Samhal prepares to sleep. I go back to the computer to nitpick at recently observed imperfections of my essays. If I don't fix or note them now, I'll forget to do it tomorrow.

"Gotta get it right or you get left out, nigga[5]." Some call me a perfectionist. Eh, I won't deny it.

All of a sudden I hear my grandma wailing again. Except this time it's louder, nonsensical and panicked. She's yelling for somebody to help. Her shrieks are a siren in our three bedroom apartment. I hustle to her bedroom where she lays under the covers of her bed. I sigh and gently shake her. I whisper-yell, "Hiwot, Hiwot, Hiwot" until she snaps out of her nightmare and quiets down into an exhausted relief. She has these traumatic episodes in her sleep almost every two weeks.

When I was in middle school, I asked Mama why Hiwot does this. She told me a long time ago one of Hiwot's neighbors was raped by her husband, so Hiwot relentlessly screamed for the other neighbors' help and rescue. I wasn't told how this despicable crime ended, but one can imagine. In Fik'ada—which is less than 10 miles from the treacherous Ethiopia-Eritrea border—neighbors are separated by their acres of farmland. Thus, when one is in danger, it is customary to scream a rhythmic caw which travels farther than a rooster's crow. Done at specific pitch and frequency, I swear it miraculously achieves resonance with the air. No technology. It's that indigenous knowledge—ancient science, truly.

But to be honest, I feel like Mama told me the watered down version of the trauma. From my research of Ethiopian history, I know Adey Hiwot lived through the Eritrean War of Independence—a 29 year-long conflict from 1961-1991 with an estimated death toll of 215,000 [15]. She also lived through what is known as the Second *Woyane* ("revolution")—a 17 year-long rebellion from 1974-1991, which included the Ethiopian Red Terror... estimated death toll: 750,000 [13]. And then, she survived the 1998-2000 Eritrean-Ethiopian Border War, which had an estimated death toll of 300,000 [16]. Mind you, through

[5] Nipsey Hussle, "Stressed Out" (2016)

all this, Hiwot never moved from her birthplace, Fik'ada, located in the famed Agamé region of Tigray, Ethiopia. Did I mention she also home-birthed 8 children, including my mom?

Despite Agamé directly translating to "fruitful" in Tigrinya, Adey Hiwot faced three different famines: the 1958 famine in her province of Tigray (estimated death toll: 100,000 [17]); the 1973 famine of Ethiopia's northern provinces (estimated death toll: 200,000 [17]); and the 1983-1985 Tigray Famine (estimated death toll: 1,200,000 [17]). Knowing this, it makes sense why her prayers before meals last as long it takes me to wolf everything down.

It wasn't until 2021, when I was 23 years old, that it dawned on me what this woman lived through: wars, famines, and God knows what else. I had already respected her as an elder and our family's matriarch, but it elevated to an exaltation and admiration of her.

When I first met Hiwot at the Los Angeles airport in 2009, the first thing I noticed about her was the sunkenness of her eyes. I'll never forget the jaw-dropping moment in 2022 when I learned sunken eyes can be a symptom of general malnutrition [18]. I've never dared to ask her directly about the famines, nor can I, because I'm still not fluent in Tigrinya. I guess it's also possible the three famines never directly affected her and she was one of the "lucky" ones.

Her plight led me to wonder: what does it take for a human to withstand such turbulence? Surely, if I can discover the blueprint for resiliency, then I can overcome anything I undergo, right?

Think of yourself as a temple under eternal construction. Over the course of your life, you gradually renovate and improve your temple. It's never complete. There's always something to build, fix, or remove.

Most of us understand—yet still underestimate—how when constructing any building, one must ensure a stable foundation. It's simple mathematics: the stronger your foundation, the longer it will last. Look no further than the Egyptian pyramids, the Great Wall of China, and the medieval European palaces as obvious examples.

Going through college is no different. It is absolutely imperative you take the time, ideally before or early in college, to solidify your personal foundation.

A foundation is something that cannot be readily destroyed. Physical foundations are typically found below ground level, hence their intrinsic indestructibility unless by act of God. Likewise, our personal foundations are typically found deeper than surface level, in a place that is accessible by only you and the Spirit.

So what can one's personal foundation contain? Let's think of the things no one can take away from us. No one can take away your name, ancestry, and ethnicity. Even more so, no one can take away your values, beliefs, and experiences. There may be more you can think of. Your personal foundation is NOT anything material or monetary. Don't be fooled. Who are you? What makes you, you?

In the case of Adey Hiwot, I came to the conclusion her foundation is extremely solid thanks to her religious beliefs and faith in God. For instance, turbulent events that would normally cause complete destruction of her temple only resulted in repairable damages. And even if a tragic event did demolish what she had, she could always rebuild on the same solid foundation. It didn't matter if someone took her food, dignity, or safety. She always possesses her power and faith through God.

If you prefer to build your own atheistic foundation from scratch, that's okay too. But you better make sure you take the time and energy to document then solidify what you stand on. Otherwise you will fall like a house in a mudslide.

What are your personal tenets? Do you subscribe to a particular doctrine? How do you hold yourself accountable of your own thoughts and actions? Are your principles readily accessible in writing for you to review? Religions and philosophies are the easiest way to answer these questions because the foundations have already been built. Like a YouTube channel, it's up to you to subscribe and engage.

But subscription and engagement to a belief is not sufficient. Just because you're of a certain religion or philosophy doesn't mean you're guaranteed success. Just because you follow a fitness influencer on Instagram doesn't mean you will lose weight or gain muscle mass. The subscription is merely a starting point, aka a foundation. It's up to you to build on it. Building your own life sounds daunting. How do we build ourselves up?

For me, I have found a simple and effective strategy: Pray First.

To the best of my ability, before I conduct any activity, I try to squeeze in a quick and silent prayer to God. Whether I'm about to drive, eat, take a test, or just starting my day, I supplicate for whatever I am in need of at the given moment.

I'm explaining this as if it's a novel idea, but it's something almost every country besides America is familiar with. This is because America's foundation was built on secularism, the separation of church and state.

You can think of your thoughts as prayers. So in a way, everything starts with a prayer and is eventually manifested if God wills it. My journey through Cal Poly started with a prayer during a time I vividly remember.

Spring 2016

It's my senior year of high school and I am starting to receive application results from different universities. I'm waiting on acceptances or rejections from ten schools, all in California, most for the major of electrical engineering. I know I want to be far from home but not too far. Plus in-state tuition is more affordable. On paper, I think my applications are pretty strong:

- 4.34 weighted GPA (5.0 scale)
- 3.7 unweighted GPA (4.0 scale)
- 1880 out of 2400 SAT score (1250 out of 1600)
- 100 volunteer hours
- Varsity basketball team captain

The parts of my applications I feel least confident about are my essays because I didn't get professional help on them. The University of California (UC) schools and private schools all require essays, while California's state schools don't. It's a nerve-wracking wait, but by April 1st, 2016, I receive all my application results. I have one month to decide where I want to take my talents. In order from dream school to "safety" school, my college applications went like this:

School	Result
1. Stanford University	Reject
2. UC Los Angeles (UCLA)	Reject
3. UC Berkeley ("Cal")	Reject
4. UC Santa Barbara (UCSB)	Reject
5. California Polytechnic State Univ. (Cal Poly)	Accept
6. Santa Clara University (SCU)	Accept
7. Loyola Marymount University (LMU)	Accept
8. University of San Diego (USD)	Accept
9. San Jose State University (SJSU)	Accept
10. San Diego State University (SDSU)	Accept
11. California State Univ. Northridge (CSUN)	Accept

Table 4.1: List of the 11 California universities that accepted me and rejected me, in order from my "dream" schools to "safety" schools.

With the ball now in my court, I narrow down the biggest decision of my life to two schools: California Polytechnic State University (Cal Poly San Luis Obispo) and Santa Clara University (SCU).

Both are to study electrical engineering (EE) and I've visited both campuses already. Cal Poly's EE bachelor's program is top ten in the nation for schools with no doctorate programs. SCU's EE program is respected and situated 15 minutes from Silicon Valley. Cal Poly is located halfway between Los Angeles and San Francisco, and it's near the beach which I love. SCU, a private school, is offering me a 4-year scholarship covering about 90% of my tuition. Cal Poly, a state school, is offering me $0 in scholarship money.

My heart is telling me Cal Poly because I think I'd be more happy with the surrounding nature and less distracting location. My brain is telling me Santa Clara because I'd basically have no student loan debt by graduation, versus an estimated $25,000 of debt at Cal Poly. I'm torn on deciding where to go, so I revise my bedtime prayers. I pray and ask God for a sign or some wisdom to help me make the best decision for me.

A week goes by and I'm sitting alone in our living room thinking about life when I have an epiphany. I realize I do not want to live a life dependent on money, but rather a life dependent on happiness. I internalize this abstract life goal, and the decision becomes a no-brainer. I choose Cal Poly and never look back.

—

Reflecting on this prayer-turned-decision, I am extremely glad it went the way it did. Overall, while at Cal Poly for 5 years, I can confidently say I was a happy person, despite several challenges I faced. I think you'll agree as you read my narrative, that I did well in college considering my circumstances and the resources at my disposal.

My time at Cal Poly was unreal. I accomplished a wide spectrum of goals while overcoming several significant trials and tribulations. Had I gone to Santa Clara University, I am almost certain I would have been less accomplished, and—even worse—less happy with my life.

It is my belief that my successes at Cal Poly all originated from that single prayer. I truly believe this, and I can attribute my inclination to pray first to my family's religious tradition—especially that of Adey Hiwot.

But as you know, faith and hope are not taught in public schools in America. Big Sean said it[6] best: "I didn't learn faith in school but that's what I'm tested on the most." Faith and its fruits are the most abstract and mysterious of personal

[6]Big Sean, "Sunday Morning Jetpack" (2017)

foundations. In fact, it does not require any academic knowledge whatsoever. It is something inscribed in our hearts and souls, and for us to discover.

For these reasons I present faith as the foremost foundational layer to navigating any challenge in life, in this case college. I hope you consider your faith as you build your life in college.

In case you're curious, here's the nightly prayer (to the best of my memory), that was the catalyst to my positive trajectory in college.

4.1 *Nightly Supplication* (Prayer)

> *In the name of the Father, the Son, and the Holy Spirit, one God, Amen. God, thank You for food, family, and friends. God, please forgive me of my sins, as You know I'm not perfect. God, please bless me so I may have the wisdom to decide which college is best for me. God, if possible, I ask that You show me a sign which will direct me towards the path that is meant for me in this world. God, please bless me with determination, motivation, perseverance, and again wisdom. God, please bless me to the fullest extent. God, please bless me so I can sleep well tonight and wake up tomorrow to take on the day. In the name of the Father, the Son, and the Holy Spirit, one God, Amen.*

Part II

FRESHMAN

I think my grandma pulled some strings on the low.
That's between her and the Lord, I'll never know.

Big K.R.I.T., "Dreamin" (2011)

5
Mentality is Paramount

Not too many people know about it, but high school students in California (and probably some other states) are eligible to take community college courses for free! The only catch is you're last on the registration priority list—but hey, if there are still some open classes, I think it's an amazing opportunity depending on the student. The stakes are low because you're not required to transfer the classes to the college you end up attending. Plus, you get a taste of what college feels like, which could be a nice confidence boost for your first quarter or semester.

When my older cousins told me about this free possibility, I went to my high school counselor and she helped direct me to the appropriate resources to make it a reality. I ended up enrolling in an unorthodox hybrid of community college, undergraduate education, and graduate schooling. Most students do two to four years of community college then transfer to complete another two to three years at a "four-year" school. Instead, I ended up using six out of my eight summer breaks—from high school through graduate school—to enroll in at least one summer course that would count towards my Cal Poly degrees.

Technically, I've been in college since the summer of 2013 (15 years old). I graduated with my bachelor's and master's degrees in the summer of 2021 (23 years old). Here's what my summer course loads looked like:

Summer Term	**School**	**Classes**
2013	Moorpark College	Intro to Engineering
2014	Moorpark College	Intro to Speech; Principles of Macroeconomics
2015	None	None
2016	None	None
2017	Foothill College	Intro to Art
2018	Foothill College	Intro to Pop Culture; American Cinema
2019	Moorpark College	Intro to Biology
2020	Cal Poly	Statistical Methods for Engineers; Data Structures

Table 5.1: List of college courses I took during my summers in high school and at Cal Poly.

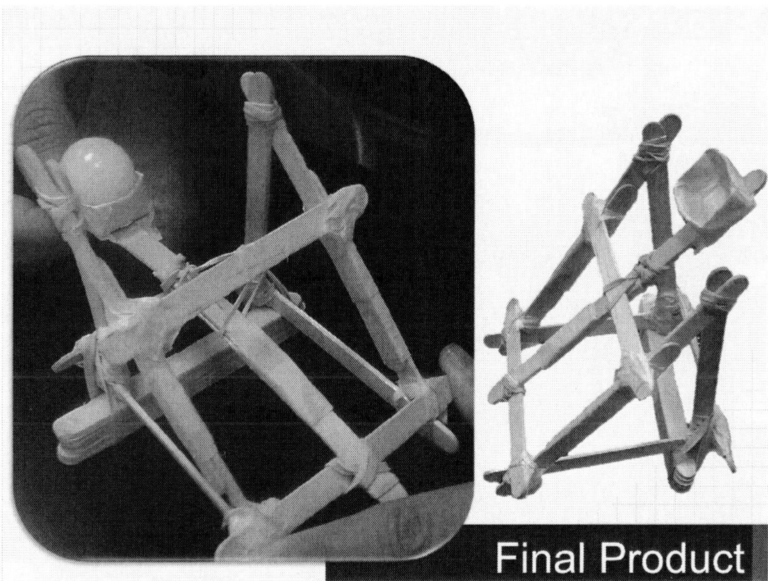

Figure 5.1: Screenshot of the concluding slide to my first ever engineering project: a popsicle stick catapult. It was built in one week by three students and myself in the Intro to Engineering class at Moorpark Community College. Summer after 9th grade. June 2013. Moorpark, California, USA.

Just to be clear, I took these classes voluntarily and not because I needed to retake classes. This uncommon strategy of spreading my courses out into most of my summer breaks was a major key to my academic successes. I prefer to do things at a manageable and constant pace with minimal breaks, rather than sprinting and taking prolonged breaks. This helps contribute to a healthy mentality. I know my limits mentally and physically, so I try to accommodate my life to fit my limits.

Do NOT try to accommodate or arrange your college life based on the capabilities or example of others! Boy did I learn this the hard way. Discover yourself. Determine what is too little and too much for you to handle. Our world's systems and standards are not a one-size-fits-all.

Cal Poly is on the quarter system, which means courses end in ten weeks instead of 16 weeks, and there are more courses in a school year. Thus, the pace of the quarter system is significantly faster than the semester system. Taking courses over the summers allowed me to slow the pace down during the normal academic school year at Cal Poly. But I guess it wasn't slow enough...

Fall Quarter, 2016

My confidence going into Cal Poly is high. It's the start of my first quarter (September 2016) and I already have 12 units graded with a 3.63 GPA. This is from the free community college courses I took during my summer breaks in high school. My weighted high school GPA was a 4.34 so I know nothing other than academic success.

I am enrolled in 14 units of classes: General Physics 1A, Calculus II, Healthy Living, and Intro to Electrical Engineering (lecture and lab). Cal Poly automatically blocked me into those courses, as they do with all freshmen in their first quarter. I'm excited. I finally get to break away from my parents and be free.

The first week of the quarter—notoriously dubbed "syllabus week"—is a breeze academically. I have it especially easy this quarter because my physics and calculus classes are only lectures, not labs. Week 4 comes around and I have my first exam at Cal Poly: physics. I think I've studied enough. After all, I did take AP Physics just last year in high school, so I should be fine, right?

Nope. Scores come back and I get a D-, well below the class average. Then, my scores come back on my first calculus exam: F, again below the class average.

Hmmm... this is no bueno. Maybe I just have bad professors? Should I study harder? I'm not in panic mode, though I do recognize this as a red flag. But eh, I already have a 3.63 GPA from my community college classes. This GPA cushion comforts me and I decide to continue with my academics as I please. I always attend my classes—that's a non-negotiable for me—and I turn in all my homework assignments to the best of my honest ability, but I never go to office hours.

My Healthy Living (kinesiology) class is a general education (GE) course so it seems pretty straightforward. My electrical engineering lecture and lab are even easier—fun, in fact—because they are meant to gently introduce you to the electrical engineering major at Cal Poly. Both the lecture and lab are worth only 1 unit each, whereas the rest of my classes are 4 units each.

The next round of exams come around during week 7. I take these exams a little more seriously. The results come back, and once again I perform below average in my physics, calculus, *and* kinesiology classes. Shit.

I'm a bit screwed for the infamous "finals week", which is during the eleventh and final week of the quarter. If I don't perform well on my final exams, I *will* have to retake classes. This is not an option. I can't give my parents any reason to force me back home. Plus, I mapped out an ambitious academic track for the next four years at Cal Poly, and I can't afford to be set back in any class.

At this point, I'm not even striving to get an A or B in physics and calculus. I'm simply trying to scrape by with a passing grade (C- or better). The week before finals week is what Cal Poly students dub "dead week", because you're overwhelmed with submitting end-of-quarter assignments as well as preparing for final exams. Desperate for results, I decide the best thing to do in between dead week and finals week is put in multiple 13-hour shifts on the quietest floor of the library. With my phone on do not disturb, the only breaks I give myself are to go to the bathroom and order food on the second floor café. At least the view is nice on the fifth floor.

The majority of my focus is directed towards studying for physics and calculus because I underestimate kinesiology—a GE course. My electrical engineering lecture and lab have no final exam, so I only have three finals. Each one is a brutal three hours long. I'm sleeping about 4-5 hours per night. Finals week comes and goes like the blink of an eye, and just like that, my first quarter at Cal Poly is complete. Here's how I did:

Class	**Units**	**Grade**
Calculus II	4	C-
General Physics 1A	4	C
Healthy Living	4	B-
Intro to EE (Lecture)	1	A
Intro to EE (Lab)	1	A

Table 5.2: My 1st quarter report card. Quarter GPA: 2.40.

Thankfully, I did well enough to pass my classes. I don't have to worry about breaking any bad news to my parents during winter break, thank God. What sucks though is that my overall GPA dropped from a 3.63 to 2.97. Ouch. So much for that community college GPA cushion.

During my three week long winter break I take the time to refocus and recalibrate. I'm not too shook by my poor academic performance. High school basketball taught me to bounce back after a bad shot, quarter, or game. So that's what I do. I shake off this anomaly of a quarter and give myself some grace—because they say majoring in electrical engineering is hard anyway!

Winter Quarter, 2017

I enter winter quarter refreshed and motivated to redeem myself academically. This quarter I picked my schedule so I'm taking classes in the mornings which is what I prefer. I even enroll in a unitless calculus workshop to supplement my studies. Besides Calculus III (4 units) and General Physics II (4 units), I'm also enrolled in Technical Writing for Engineers (4 units), Basic Electronics Manufacturing (2 units), and California Constitution & Government (1 unit). It's one more unit than last quarter, but I'm ready.

During the quarter, I meet an engineering academic advisor named Meghan. It's her first year at Cal Poly too, and she periodically asks me how classes are going because she sees all the quarter grades I earn. In a venting fashion, I always update her on my academics.

As the academic term proceeds, I do marginally better than the previous quarter. I'm not getting any A's or B's on exams, but I hover near or below the class averages. Winter quarter flies by faster than fall. Before I know it, finals come and go. Here's how I did:

Class	**Units**	**Grade**
Calculus III	4	C+
General Physics II	4	C+
Tech Writing for Engineers	4	A
Basic Electronics Manufacturing	2	A-
California Constitution & Government	1	B

Table 5.3: My 2nd quarter report card. Quarter GPA: 2.99.

Almost a 3.0 quarter GPA! What a sigh of relief. I'm back onto a positive trajectory. It's still not where I want to be, but I'm content with the results. I knew college wouldn't be that bad. After this, I'll do even better—it only makes sense. The next logical step is for me to obtain "Dean's List" status next quarter, which is a 3.5 GPA. Although a 3.5 GPA means averaging an A- grade in all my classes, I still set it as a goal because I don't shy away from ambitious endeavors.

Spring Quarter, 2017

Not only do I have a goal, but I have a plan to get there. Thanks to a conference I attended during spring break, I plan to implement an extremely structured strategy called the "Guaranteed 4.0 Learning System". The Guaranteed 4.0 plan requires one to plan out each hour of their week, to the best of their ability.

Determined to reach the coveted Dean's List, I follow the plan religiously. I buy a new binder and folders, as instructed. I block out each hour of my weekly calendar so it has a purpose. I allot time for everything one would need to live a healthy life: studying, eating, exercise, sleep, class, leisure, etc.

I am set up for success. I'm not expecting the advertised "guaranteed 4.0", but surely I must get close to it. This is exactly what I need because I hear spring quarters at Cal Poly are supposed to be the most fun: warm weather, the beach 15 minutes away, and parties galore—the California college dream.

My spring schedule is a doozy though. 14 units of pure pain: Calculus IV (4 units), General Physics III (4 units), Fundamentals of Computer Science (4 units), and Electric Circuits Analysis (2 units). Math, science, coding, and engineering classes all in one quarter. I would never wish this burden on any student. I don't know how I'm expected to retain knowledge taking all these courses at once. Isn't the point of college to retain information for use in the future?

Anyway, this brutal spring schedule is another reason why I need the Guaranteed 4.0 plan—especially if I want to enjoy the spring quarter like I hear I should.

I'm back on campus and begin implementing the novel strategy. It includes a sophisticated note taking plan—before, during, and after every single lecture. It's difficult, but I try.

The problem is, unforeseen stuff keeps coming up and disrupting my blocked-out schedule. And sometimes, I'm just not in the mood or mindset to take notes. What am I supposed to do when I become surprisingly hungry and unexpectedly tired?

The first round of exams arrive and the results are in. 84% in calculus, 87% in electric circuits, and 91% in computer science. Pretty good! The only exception is my physics class which has no exams, just weekly quizzes in which my average score is an F.

The second round of exams hit hard and now the prospects of passing my classes is in jeopardy: 64% in calculus, 81% in computer science, and more F's on my weekly physics quizzes.

Uh oh. Not again. Nope. This is not happening. Time to go into overdrive and bounce back. I try to double down on the Guaranteed 4.0 plan, but I'm not going to lie, it feels like extreme turbulence on a flight and I'm the pilot. I'm trying my best to stick to the preset path and land somewhere nearby the Dean's List tarmac. A 4.0 is for surely not on my radar. Neither is Dean's List.

I am low-key in full blown panic mode now. My self-piloted flight has no other option than to make an unplanned emergency landing. In fact, I abandon the Guaranteed 4.0 plan entirely. There's no way it'll work at this point, and there's no time in the quarter to evaluate and reassess—I'll do that in the summer. So, I resort back to the academic regimen that feels natural to me.

Besides me being young and irresponsible this spring quarter, it also doesn't help that my physics professor is the worst teacher I've ever had up to this point of my life because he's soon-to-retire and super unorganized. My calculus professor is solid, but an unforgiving grader, and my computer science professor is below average, but thankfully, my roommate's older brother is helping me through it. I'm not too worried about computer science because it's mainly project-based, so I can pull all-nighters to get through. My concern is once again calculus, and especially physics.

Dead week is upon me and I decide to put in more 13-hour shifts at the library since that worked for me last quarter. I get a few hours of sleep each night. I do my best on my final exams and await the results. I am absolutely dreading the release of the grades. I'm already back home with my parents, and I don't want to break any bad news to them. I fear I may need to retake both calculus and physics classes which will cost more money and time.

The angst is so real. The hour finally comes for me to check my grades. Here's how I did:

Class	**Units**	**Grade**
Calculus IV	4	D+
General Physics III	4	D
Fundamentals of Computer Science	4	B
Electric Circuits Analysis	2	A-

Table 5.4: My 3rd quarter report card. Quarter GPA: 1.90.

As a freshman, I took fall quarter as an uppercut to the chin, winter quarter as a strike to the gut, and spring quarter as a blow below the belt. Fall quarter tested my psyche and confidence. Winter quarter made me second guess myself. And spring quarter?... Damn, those grades broke my academic heart.

With a pathetic 1.9 quarter GPA, my overall GPA plunges to 2.44. Wow. Not only did I entirely miss my goal of Dean's

List, but I managed to land on uncharted territory known as "Academic Probation". I have never heard of this before. It's when you obtain less than a 2.0 term GPA. If it happens again next quarter, I'll be kicked out of Cal Poly. Fuck, man.

This is the lowest point of my academic career and is a true test of my ambitions. I take full responsibility of my poor performance, but I have to at least try to get my grades bumped up. I send kind and desperate emails to both my professors. The physics professor never replies. The calculus professor responds informing me that I earned a dismal 51% on my final exam—well below the class average of 76%. Damn.

I guess I have to retake calculus and physics. I begin to look into what I need to do in order to switch up my schedule for next quarter. Reading the fine print, I find that a C- is needed to matriculate into subsequent calculus or physics courses. As an electrical engineering student, these spring courses were the last calculus and general physics classes I needed. It did not specify what is needed to "pass" if you're at the end of a series of classes.

I must be overlooking something so I respond to a "checking in" email from my now favorite academic counselor, Meghan, and she confirms what I read. In this specific circumstance, I needed at least a D- to pass each class. Wow. I don't have to retake any classes!

This, my friend, is why they say "D's get degrees".

Summer Quarter, 2017

After a brief sigh of relief, it's time for me to face the reality of my disastrous academic school year. I'm at a crossroads. Since it's my summer break, I have time to ruminate. For brief moments, I wonder:

Should I change majors? Maybe I should change schools? Do I have what it takes to be an engineer? Is it because I'm

Black at a PWI? Is this all even worth it? Why am I in school? Why not just give up on academics? Am I inferior? Do I matter?...

I don't know what it is, but this negative thinking is a downward spiral to failure. Later in college, I learn this phenomenon is called "imposter syndrome".

I drive to Zuma Beach in Malibu because the ocean calms me. After hypothesizing what I did wrong and how I need to change, I make a pact with myself. I realize it doesn't necessarily start with my study habits or time management. It starts with my mentality.

My new mental pact and mind state is to always strive to obtain a higher cumulative GPA than the previous quarter. Simple as that.

No institutionally-set GPA goals. No comparing myself to my classmates. No comparing myself to the class average. No pressure from my parents' expectations. None of that. From here on out, I will only try to do better than my previous self.

Besides, the traditional letter-based grading system is outdated. How could one grading system work to accurately assess *all* students? GPA does not matter when all is said and done. A GPA is only enough to get your foot in the door—it won't take you any farther than that. Your GPA is an merely an imprecise indicator with an appreciable amount of error. In fact, did you know several colleges in the United States have abandoned letter grading and instead use alternative grading systems [19]?

—

My new mentality proved successful, because over the next three years, my cumulative undergraduate GPA gradually improved to a 3.0. Here's how it looked:

Figure 5.2: My undergraduate GPA's positive trajectory after I changed my mentality. Freshman to Senior year, final undergraduate GPA: 3.0.

My adjusted mentality was the second layer of foundation I needed on top of my faith. Overall, it was a healthy mentality because I recognized that some practices could be toxic—even within our "world-class" educational institutions. I tried to avoid or limit anything which I deemed cancerous for my mind. Toxic competitiveness was one of them. Imposter syndrome was another.

A healthy mentality is what got me through all my "weed-out" courses at Cal Poly. The first and second years at every university are often loaded with weed-out courses meant to sift out those who are not fit for the cut. Sure, it does add some prestige and high standards to academic programs, but it also is unnecessarily taxing on students.

"Healthy mentality" will look different for everyone. And sometimes the circumstances around us do not allow for such a healthy mentality. For example, one could have trauma-inducing family members, triggering roommates, neurodivergencies, excessive substance usage, a microaggressive community, or medically diagnosed diseases, amongst many other challenges.

If you feel as though you cannot create your own healthy psyche, then that's okay! That's what psychiatrists, therapists, support groups, friends, and religions are here to help us with. They can help pinpoint areas of toxicity within our lives, and then can assist in cleansing or healing said toxicity.

Don't ever be afraid to seek mental health support. It may be closer than you think. I'm not only talking about going to a psychiatrist. I'm also talking about simple things like asking anyone—even a stranger—for a hug! Be gentle with yourself, my friend. Our minds are more fragile than our bodies.

Personally, I treat my mental health just like my physical health, with care and proactiveness. Similar to how people are cautious with what they eat, I beware of the things I view, hear, touch, and smell. On social media I try to mute or unfollow content which I deem unhealthy for my mind. On streaming platforms, I try to listen to music which aligns with my values or supports my goals (see Table 5.5 at the end of this chapter). In public and private, I try to touch with caution and restraint. Under peer pressure, I try not to sniff or snort anything other than oxygen.

Those weed-out courses like calculus, physics, and chemistry took a toll on my mind and body. They defeated me. So it is not enough to have only a solid foundation of faith and healthy mentality, but there is a third foundational layer necessary for completing college: community.

While I struggled academically in my freshman year, I managed to thrive socially, which fortified my mentality. I can't describe my first year of college without discussing the community which cultivated around me.

5.1 *Food4Thought* (Playlist)

Table 5.5: A three-hour-long music playlist I made titled, "Food4Thought" [7], which I listened to while struggling mentally as an underclassman.

***Food4Thought* Playlist [7]**	
Artist(s)	**Song Title**
Fabolous & Jadakiss	Talk About It (feat. Teyana Taylor)
Big K.R.I.T.	Another Naive Individual Glorifying Greed and Encouraging Racism
Kendrick Lamar	F*ck Your Ethnicity
YG	Blacks & Browns (feat. Sad Boy)
Jace	J.A.N.
Joey Bada$$	TEMPTATION
Nipsey Hussle	50 Niggaz
Logic	Take it Back
Meek Mill	Stay Woke (feat. Miguel)
Meek Mill	Oodles O'Noodles Babies
Frank Ocean	Crack Rock
Common	It's Your World, Pts. 1 & 2
Ace Hood	Black (Skit)
Ace Hood	Mr. Black Man
Westside Boogie	Further

Food4Thought Playlist[7]	
Artist(s)	**Song Title**
The Game	The Ghetto (feat. Nas & will.i.am)
2Pac	Brenda's Got a Baby
A Tribe Called Quest	Conrad Tokyo
Belly	Immigrant (feat. Meek Mill & M.I.A.)
Kendrick Lamar	untitled 03 | 05.28.2013
Dr. Dre	Animals (feat. Anderson .Paak)
Cordae	Target
Meek Mill	Young Black America (feat. The Dream)
J. Cole	Caged Bird (feat. Omen)
J. Cole	Chaining Day
Isaiah Rashad	Ronnie Drake (feat. SZA)
Joey Bada$$	GOOD MORNING AMERIKKKA
Meek Mill	These Scars (feat. Future & Guordan Banks)
The Notorious B.I.G.	Juicy
Ty Dolla $ign	No Justice (feat. Big TC)
TeeCee4800	25 to Life
Kendrick Lamar	Uncle Bobby & Jason Keaton (feat. Javonte)
JAY-Z	My President is Black
YG	FDT (feat. Nipsey Hussle)
YG	FDT, Pt. 2 (feat. G-Eazy & Macklemore)
Childish Gambino	This Is America

Food4Thought Playlist[7]	
Artist(s)	**Song Title**
Kendrick Lamar	Institutionalized (feat. Bilal, Anna Wise & Snoop Dogg)
Kendrick Lamar	Complexion (A Zulu Love) [feat. Rapsody]
The Game	Magnus Carlsen (feat. Anderson .Paak)
Vince Staples	Summertime
Kendrick Lamar	The Blacker The Berry
Big K.R.I.T.	The Alarm
Logic	AfricAryaN (feat. Neil deGrasse Tyson)
Joey Bada$$	AMERIKKKAN IDOL
Lil Wayne	DontGetIt
45 songs, 3 hours and 15 minutes	

"For acceptance, niggas will do anything."
J. Cole, "Window Pain (Outro)" (2018)

6
We Long to Belong

Fall Quarter, 2016

Truth is, I was all over the place freshman year. Parties, employment, workshops, volunteering, sports, traveling—you name it, I probably did it. I don't recommend my abnormally high level of involvement because your grades may be compromised as mine were. That said, I have absolutely no regrets.

Throughout college, I was an ambivert—equally introverted and extroverted—according to online personality tests. I enjoy being with people just as much as I enjoy being alone. My underclassman days definitely brought out the extrovert in me.

My very first community at Cal Poly was my dormitory floor. There were twelve dorm rooms with about 30 male-identifying students on my floor. We were on the third and top floor of Sierra Madre Tower 1.

My roommate was my good high school friend, Adam, who I first met through basketball. A stocky lefty, we bonded in high school in many ways, such as eating free pizza from his Rabbi's weekly Jewish Student Union (JSU) meetings. I went because I liked the kosher pizza, Rabbi Bryski, and my friends who all went too. Thousand Oaks High School had nothing organized specifically for Black students at the time.

One of the reasons I ended up picking Cal Poly over Santa Clara University was thanks to Adam's generosity. During the second semester of our senior year of high school, he invited me to a weekend stay with his older brother who studied Computer Science at Cal Poly. That spring weekend gave me a taste of what my college life could look like.

On top of this, Adam got early admission acceptance from Cal Poly, which meant he was first priority for the more desirable two-person dorms. Meanwhile, I was accepted during the regular admission time frame. Eventually, we mutually agreed to select each other as preferred roommates which meant that I upgraded from the three-person to two-person dorm rooms—a huge step up in terms of personal space and privacy.

But Adam and I didn't lean on each other too much. We both did our own things as the year went on, which was nice. Our all-male floor was lit. Within the first three weeks of school, we quickly became known by the neighboring dormitories as the party floor. This was before anyone could rush Greek life, let alone legally buy a beer, so we turned our common areas into a club—colored LED lights and everything.

In fact, our floor had its own Instagram page and the bio was "bitches on the tables, boys on the couches... Striving for Litness. Documenting Greatness." Yup.

Well, that didn't last long because by Halloween weekend (around week 5), the residential advisors (RA's) were so fed up with us that they called in the university police, who pulled up on us SWAT-style during a little function. No, seriously. Our dormitory floor only had two entry/exit points: one stairwell on the west side and another on the east side. They simultaneously sent one officer and an RA up each stairwell so they could corner the rambunctious north side common area.

The 20 or so students began to scramble to hide in random dorm rooms. The police waited and yelled for everyone to come out immediately. Eventually, everyone complied and they scolded the group, threatening folks with academic consequences.

Naturally, I—the only Black student—evaded this trapping of the common area. As soon as I caught wind the RA's were coming back for the third time that night, my instincts told me something was up. Just as the police paraded in, I wisely entered the communal bathroom which has two entry/exit points. I waltzed out the other bathroom door and into safety in the south side common area where my room was. Come on now.

Albeit degenerate, we had a community. Late night common area chats, nonstop PlayStation FIFA battles, watching pro sports, and even following the United States presidential election...

On the evening of November 9th, 2016 (around week 7), everyone in the country was glued to the news. Who would be America's next president? Hillary Clinton or Donald Trump?

Adam had a nice 40-inch flatscreen TV set up in our dorm, and so did our friends within sight across the hall. Both TVs were blaring—one with CNN, the other with Fox News. We were all at least a little anxious to hear the final outcome.

As we watched CNN's John King do his thing, Ethan's room across the hall burst into a boastful chant of woohoo's and yippee's. Fox News predicted Donald Trump won the election.

Up 'til that point no one on the floor talked much politics or revealed their stance. But seeing and hearing the reactions of my various floormates said it all.

After Trump's victory, and for the rest of the year, the country music from Ethan's room seemed just a bit louder, the American flag just a bit more visible, and the cowboy-like attire just a bit more regular. That stung.

For the rest of the school year, I kept the peace on the floor, although we all recognized and accepted our polarizing differences. Besides, people began to find their communities outside the dorm floor, so we all slowly grew apart as the year went on anyway.

I've come to realize that having not-so-ideal neighbors is not unique to college, but rather a part of life. No matter where you move there is bound to be someone nearby who rubs you the wrong way or even worse is your enemy. Thus, it's best to learn how to live amongst all people because "your own profit lies in the profit of your neighbor, and his in yours."[1].

A manager at a summer internship once told me, "good fences make good neighbors," and I'll never forget it. Following this advice will suit you well in your neighborhood, workplace, and relationships.

Before I moved to sunny San Luis Obispo, I already knew of two extracurriculars I wanted to do: intramural basketball refereeing and high school basketball refereeing. When I was in high school I worked as a youth basketball referee for four years. Basketball was my passion and the job paid me in cash, $20 per game. It was good pocket money for a high schooler and I wanted to continue this healthy hustle in college.

[1]"The Love Chapter" by St. John Chrysostom.

I already had connections with the high school reffing association in Ventura county through various mentors. In fact, I completed their two-month certification program only to be denied work because I was still a senior in high school, creating a conflict of interest. Nevertheless, I set up the pieces to transfer into the reffing association in San Luis Obispo county.

This new reffing association was a cohort of about 80 officials—the majority of them men older than 50. I was the youngest referee in the association. Despite the age gap with my on-court partners, I worked well with everyone to officiate boys and girls basketball games of all levels except varsity. The pay was $64 per 90-minute game and I worked anywhere from 1-4 games per week during basketball season. It was good, efficient money. I worked this off-campus job as a freshman and sophomore with basketball seasons running annually from November through March.

Officiating high school basketball didn't provide me a tight-knit community by any means, but it did allow me to interact with the surrounding residents of the county, which was still valuable. All my referee partners mentored me through my rookie and sophomore seasons. Imagine meeting up with a local adult stranger and effectively officiating a game for random local children while their family members watch the whole thing... If that ain't a form of cohesive community, I don't know what is!

Over time, I became a favorite of many of the high school players—mainly because I was young like them, but also because white people love to fetishize Black people on basketball courts. Either before, during, or after games, the students often asked me if I could dunk for them or if I played basketball for some team.

The coaches respected me because I was honest and fair, but some tried to bully me because of my inexperience. The fans never seemed to have a problem with me. If they did, it was them frustrated with my partner slacking. Even years after I retired from officiating, several high schoolers who graduated and attended Cal Poly would say, "wassup," to me if they found me playing pick-up ball on campus. I thought that was pretty neat.

The tough part about high school officiating was the travel. Depending on what the assignor scheduled me for, I would have to travel anywhere from 5 to 30 minutes to games; but sometimes I got doubleheaders which was nice. Despite making around $2,000 per basketball season, I still needed some money on a more consistent basis and in the off-season. That's why I pursued on-campus intramural basketball officiating as well.

As soon as I arrived on campus as a freshman, I made sure to find the intramural office, where I found a flyer advertising the meeting to hire intramural sports referees. I eventually was hired and earned about $13.25 per game (minimum wage in California at the time), working anywhere from 0-5 hours per week for the next 15 months. To my surprise, the job not only offered me a little paycheck, but also another little community. All the intramural student referees bonded with each other over basketball. What a pleasant surprise.

On top of that, as one of the few Black employees, players quickly began to recognize and remember me off the court, in places like class, food halls, and parties. It made me feel like the token Black guy. Nonetheless, I began to distinguish the Brads from the Chads as well.

I cannot underestimate the value of walking around a campus and recognizing the faces you see, let alone have those faces recognize you. This is one subtle manifestation of community. It is our human nature to desire to belong; to feel like we occupy a meaningful space worth noticing—to be seen, heard, acknowledged, and respected on our terms.

Let's go back to my first month at Cal Poly—before I got the job—when I was too innocent and naive to know any of this.

—

It's a comfortable October evening in San Luis Obispo. I'm wearing my knock-off Kobe Bryant jersey and the sun is soon to set. I'm an eager freshman on my way to the first intramural sports employment meeting of the quarter. I don't have too many friends on campus yet so I go alone.

My #8 Kobe jersey is an intentional fashion choice, because I'm hoping it will signal to strangers and those hiring that I like basketball and am looking to officiate it on-campus. There's about 50 people in the auditorium attached to the recreation center, and they give an attractive presentation on the requirements and responsibilities of intramural sports referees.

I'm sold on the organization, but there's one problem: I can't make it to the mandatory basketball scrimmage tomorrow evening because I have my weekly electrical engineering lab class at the same time. They want to see us at a scrimmage with a whistle so they can assess our current comfortability with basketball. Obviously, I know I'm qualified, but they need to see the proof.

Bummed, I let the basketball manager know of my conflict right before the session ends. He didn't seem impressed or convinced of my self-proclaimed expertise in basketball officiating. Damn, what a disappointment. If they don't hire me, I'll have to wait 'til next quarter to try again.

With my spirits low, I walk out the auditorium into the darkness of the night. As I'm walking up some stairs, a man's voice from behind startles me saying, "Hey, I overheard you can't make the scrimmage tomorrow?" I turn around to see a big-bodied white guy in shorts and a t-shirt. "Uh yeah, I got lab unfortunately."

He double checks, "are you really trying to ref?" I respond, "Yeah man, I love refereeing basketball. I've been doing it for the last four years."

"Okay, let me take you back inside and direct you to who you should talk to." This kind 6'6" stranger and I walk back into the auditorium and he points out the director of the organization. "Go pitch yourself to him. He's the one you want to talk to."

Before he heads out I learn his name is Brett, and I give him my sincere thanks. "No problem, man. Good luck. Oh and I love the Lakers jersey by the way."

Wow. What a friendly guy. Hopefully his advice will help. I approach the director who turns out to be the manager of the manager I talked to earlier. Perfect.

I provide him with an even more enthusiastic pitch of my self-proclaimed expertise and passion for officiating basketball. He seems much more receptive to my effort and tells me he can't make any promises but he'll see what he can do. Wonderful. That's the best I can ask for.

A week goes by and I'm notified with good news: I'm hired! Shortly after, I report to the orientation meeting alongside the other 15 students who were hired. I think I'm the only freshman—probably because this job opportunity came about so early in the fall quarter. We receive a brief training from experienced students, and then the manager assigns us next week's schedule based on our availabilities. None of this is new to me so it's quite a stress-free experience.

Another week goes by and I clock in for my first set of intramural basketball games. As fate would have it, my first game is with Brett! We officiate a smooth first half and have some time to chat during halftime.

A little small talk then he asks me, "are you planning on rushing a fraternity?" I tell him no because I'm so busy focusing on academics, work, and my career development. This week is career fair week, so there are a lot of events with opportunities to network and learn about different companies.

Brett respects it and mentions that he's in the fraternity that has had the highest average GPA in Greek Life for the past three quarters. The comment perks my interest. I guess if I *were* to ever join any fraternity here, it would be that one.

A couple days later Brett direct messages me inviting me to a Sigma Nu rush event with free barbecue. I respectfully decline because I already have plans to attend an evening info session for the oil and gas company, Phillips 66.

The next day, he kindly reaches out to me again inviting me this time to a Sigma Nu pizza mixer. Apparently it's my last chance to go for the quarter. In my household, I was taught to respect one's invitation, especially if they did something kind for you. Without Brett, I wouldn't have been hired as an intramural referee.

I take up his invitation and walk alone to an apartment just off-campus. Brett greets me at the door and takes me upstairs where the breakout mixer is happening. We arrive in a living room with about 20 students, some of them Sigma Nu members and the rest potential new members (PNM's). Brett introduces me to some current members while I eat some free hot dogs.

One thing I did *not* research before coming to college was Greek life, so I'm clueless. It never really occurred to me because I didn't think it applied to me. Plus, I'm not one to dwell on my social status or "coolness", because I know it's all a facade. Many of the "cool" people at my high school peaked in high school. The little I do know about fraternities and sororities is that they like to party and are predominantly white.

Thus, I have no preconceptions of Greek life at Cal Poly. Besides, I don't like to judge people based on assumptions. The sober mixer is nothing more than a bunch of bros "man-flirting" with each other. I meet two upperclassmen electrical engineering students named David and Arshan. It's clear they know exactly how to navigate the EE department and I note them as connections that could mentor me academically. Later, I meet the fraternity's philanthropy chair, Chris. I don't even know what the word philanthropy means, so he enlightens me on the topic and how the fraternity volunteers and donates.

Finally, I meet some guys who also play ball recreationally. They ask if I can attend the rush event tomorrow, which is an outdoor sports day. I can't because of class conflicts. The 2-hour event goes by quick since I love to talk with people. I thank Brett for the food and invite, and then walk back to my dorm. I'm not rushing any other fraternities and there are no active Black fraternities at Cal Poly.

I miss the sports day event and then receive an invitation to a subsequent invite-only rush event at the fraternity's chapter house. The agenda is to enjoy college football game-day with some burgers (and no alcohol). I decide to attend because I enjoyed the conversations I had at the mixer, and hope to meet more people who can help me get to where I want to go in life.

The invite-only event goes smooth. Over 100 people are in attendance and it smells like a backyard barbecue. I meet some more engineers and ask a lot questions about how upperclassmen navigate college and their careers. The active members provide me insight I've never heard before, and they all seem to be well-rounded individuals capable of working and playing hard. It becomes evident to me that many of these members are white or come from white-collar families. Noted.

That evening, I receive an invitation to the fraternity's last rush event: an invite-only interview day where everyone is dressed in formal attire. I have nothing to lose so I put on my suit and tie. My interview was taken seriously and tested my ability to communicate under pressure. It's not stressful for me because I was never seeking a fraternity; they were seeking me.

Another day goes by and I receive notice that out of over 400 rushees, I am one of 24 who is receiving a bid into the fraternity. If I accept the bid, then I am to partake in the months-long pledging process, which may qualify me for full initiation into the brotherhood of just over 100 men. It doesn't occur to me how cult-like this opportunity is.

I'm a little caught off-guard and surprised by this bid. Not counting interviews, I only attended two of the five rush events. Some students attend all rush events and still don't receive fraternity bids. Why would they want me? Why do they like me? How the hell have I even gotten to this point?

At this moment, I reflect. If Brett wasn't a Good Samaritan, none of this would have happened. This seems like a divine sign. There's no way this could all be an accident. There must be a reason why this opportunity plopped right on my plate. Lately, I have been asking God for signs to keep me on the path that's meant for me. Maybe this is one of those signs? If so, it is quite the switchback on my life journey.

Besides using faith and instinct, I consider the more predictable outcomes of accepting a bid. If I accept this bid, I will be tapped into a network of affluent individuals—well, affluent to me. Wealth is always relative. As the saying goes, "be wary of the company you keep for they are a reflection of who you are, or who you want to be." I think some Black folks would characterize such thinking from a Black man as "coon behavior."

Ultimately, I could use this network to my advantage, whether it be professional, academic, or social. The benefits are hard to quantify because the sky is the limit. I find this extremely attractive.

By the way, I don't care much for the clout and access to "exclusive" parties—their inclusion is welcomed as an accessory. Rather, it's all about excelling my life and career for the benefit of me and my family.

One obvious downside is the membership cost. If I make it through the pledging process, I will have to pay $400 per quarter ($1200 per academic year), and that doesn't count miscellaneous expenses of fraternity life, such as formals, fundraisers, and alcohol. Welp, there goes all of my refereeing paychecks. I would never dare to expect my parents to pay for something like this—that is not an option.

The other downside to this opportunity is the distracting nature of fraternity life. There is no doubt this new network would distract me from my academics, despite boasting the highest average GPA in Cal Poly's Greek Life... decisions, decisions.

Since I only have 24 hours to accept or decline the bid, I come to a conclusion by the following morning. I will accept the bid. I figure it can't hurt to try. Worst case scenario is I drop during the pledging process. At an uncanny bid ceremony in front of over 30 actives, I notify the Sigma Nu, Kappa Pi chapter of my acceptance, and the pledge process begins.

But wait, there's more. Let's go back to the night of the first intramural sports employment meeting.

—

Having just met Brett for the first time at the reffing meeting, I head to the university dining hall called The Avenue to eat Chik-fil-A for dinner. The hall has several flat screen TVs playing sports highlights, so I dine near them to keep me company. As I'm trying to enjoy my spicy chicken sandwich alone, a polite female voice startles me from behind, "Excuse me." I turn around and she continues, "Sorry to interrupt your meal, but I saw you from afar and have to ask: are you Habesha?"

I answer, "Yes, I'm Ethiopian!" She beams, "me too! My name is Lul." Coincidentally, she is also an engineering student. Lul, whose name means "pearl" in Tigrinya, tells me about this organization called the National Society of Black Engineers, also known as NSBE (pronounced *nezbee*). Lul grabs my number and tells me she will text me when and where the next NSBE meeting is happening.

A few days pass, and Lul texts me to come to the third floor of the construction management building at 7:10PM. With no expectations, I walk half a mile alone from my dorm to the room.

I walk into a nearly empty classroom with only five students present and it smells like a greasy Louisiana kitchen. I don't see Lul, but most everyone is fixated over a table of Popeye's, serving themselves dinner.

Some students welcome me to dinner, and the meeting commences. In total, seven students—all Black—are now present. Oddly, five of the students—wearing slick, black NSBE polos—walk to the front of the room to help present the projected slide deck. So there are only two people in the "crowd": me and another Black student. I find it quite polarizing when comparing it to the fraternity events I was just at.

Despite the quantity in attendance, I am thoroughly impressed and attracted by NSBE's quality and vision. We all recite the NSBE mission statement in unison to kick off the meeting:

> *To increase the number of culturally responsible Black engineers who excel academically, succeed*

> *professionally, and positively impact the community.*

By the end of the meeting, I'm sold on becoming a paid member. It's an easy decision for me because it doesn't seem like much of a commitment compared to how much it could offer me. Apparently, NSBE has scholarships, mentorship opportunities, free dinners at meetings, as well as two or three expenses-paid conferences a year. At a price of only $25 per year, it's a no-brainer for me.

After the meeting concludes, I meet the five-person executive board of the Cal Poly NSBE chapter. Dejah is the president, Jeana is vice president, Cash is treasurer, Averil is programs director, and Ben is secretary. Seems like a solid squad I can learn from, relate to, and get along with.

I join the NSBE group chat, email newsletter, and follow the Instagram page. My NSBE journey begins.

—

In retrospect, NSBE definitely shaped my college experience—especially my last three years. Greek life shaped my college experience as well—especially my first two years.

In my first quarter I also found community with the Black Student Union (BSU), but its presence varied due to volatility and instability. Cal Poly only had two Black organized communities while I was a student. NSBE and BSU... no fraternities or sororities from The Divine Nine.

Note how I obtained on-campus employment, joined NSBE, and began the fraternity pledging process all in my first quarter of college. In other words, I immediately was received and included by five tight-knit and organized communities at my school—albeit only two looked like me.

Good communities come with a lot of perks, by the way. Greek life got me four years of prime off-campus apartment living and good roommates. NSBE got me my first and second engineering internships as well as my first job after graduation. NSBE, BSU, and Greek life provided me with plenty of free or discounted food, drinks, and travel. I could go on and on with the benefits of community... I'll share more in detail in future publications.

Regardless of if a community looks like you or not, we all long to belong. No one in their right mind enjoys being an outcast. Deep down, we want to receive neighborly love. To receive this feeling of belonging within my first quarter of college was tremendously impactful in a positive way.

Thankfully the support beams to my personal foundation were found early and immediately ready for use.

From then on out, whether I was working, exercising, studying, socializing, or partying, I always had at least an acquaintance within reach. On campus, I no longer walked alone.

Like I mentioned in Chapter 2, *Corny Icebreakers*, the process of building friendships and community will often be awkward at first.

But I implore you to put yourself out there and seek community early and often. Your network will eventually be the people who connect to future job opportunities. Your personal "board of directors" will be the ones who influence the path you choose in life. And to bring it full circle, your community will eventually be how you positively or negatively impact others in this world.

"Aside from the faculty of reason there is also another power which has greater value: the nous, the heart."

Metropolitan of Nafpaktos Hierotheos, "Orthodox Psychotherapy", (2017)

7 Drunk Mind Speaks a Sober Heart

Spring Quarter, 2017

Weekends during spring quarter at Cal Poly are unmatched. San Luis Obispo is a retirement town for a reason. The mornings are sometimes a bit brisk, but besides that, the weather is warm during the day and lukewarm at night. No gusty winds, no surprise rain showers. Just clear blue skies with a light breeze.

My fraternity brothers and I just finished an afternoon hike of Cerro San Luis Obispo, better known as "Madonna Mountain" for its large, white M-shaped rock facing east. We grabbed sushi off-campus as a celebratory meal, then return to our homes to get ready for the night.

There's a big party tonight. It's supposed to be one of the best ones of the year, and everyone is hyping it up—as they do with every weekend party. The event is named "Snu Orleans" and the theme is Mardi Gras. I don't know what outfit would match the theme so I put on my Roscoe's House of Chicken and Waffles t-shirt with jeans and look in the dorm mirror. Mardi Gras? Eh, I don't care enough to try harder. I don't even know what Mardi Gras celebrates[1]. Ignorant.

I spruce up and prepare myself a to-go drink with my favorite alcohol: tequila. Recently, I found out I like tequila because out of all the alcohols, it's the best "liquid courage" for me. For some reason, when I drink tequila, I loosen up from my typical uptight self. I also am more likely to shoot my shot at a girl if tequila is in my system.

Sprite bottle in hand, I'm about to walk out our dorm room when Adam yells, "Yo Amman, let's take a shot." I turn around and he's already got a handle of vodka in hand, with two shot glasses, eager to serve me. Taking shots or "icing" each other is our way of bonding, I think. He has his own fraternity party to attend.

His vodka is clear and my Tequila is also clear. I hear if you stick to the same color alcohols, hangovers aren't as bad. Should I accept his offer? I don't like disappointing people and aim to stay on good terms with those around me—especially my roommate.

"I already made a tequila drink, bro. But alright, just one shot." Adam nods firmly in giddy approval. He doesn't want to drink alone, so my company appeases and justifies his desires.

One shot of Costco's Kirkland brand vodka down to the liver. I hate vodka ugh. Adam tries to convince me into another

[1] *Mardi Gras* is French for "Fat Tuesday", reflecting the practice of the last night of eating rich, fatty foods before the fasting of the Christian Lent season [20]

shot but I shut it down and head out. I head over to a pregame my pledge bros are hosting. I'm never the one to lead party plans—it's just not my nature. So I typically just go wherever I get an invite.

I quietly walk into the apartment bumping electronic dance music (EDM)—which I don't really like. "AMMMAAANN!!" the guys yell. Cheesing, I meekly reply, "Ayyyeee what's up everyone?"

Mike daps me, "what's good bro!?"

Dan bear hugs me, "so nice to see you bro."

Aidan bro hugs me, "my guy!"

I make my rounds to the roughly 15 people present. Bro hugs for the bros and half hugs for the ladies—since I'm not super close with any of them.

"Let's take a shot!" Stu belts beside me. "Haha okay, I got my drink already so let's do it." Our circle of five takes our swigs. Two shots of tequila and sprite down to my liver.

I know how to handle my alcohol relative to some of my peers. I've blacked out a couple times, but everyone says I'm pretty mellow and compliant when I do. My friends say it's hard to know whether or not I'm drunk. I take pride in my self-control even when drunk, but it also contributes to me seeming perpetually "uptight."

After some futile small talk with the lads and ladies, Preston screams, "Alright everyone let's mob to picket!" It's time for the party. "Picket," officially known as "White Picket" in the fraternity, is our top satellite house. As it's name implies, it has a quaint front yard surrounded by a classic white picket fence. It's situated at the heart of the "red zone" which is basically the most party-dense neighborhoods right off-campus. Ideal for partying, it's a one story, three bedroom, two bath home with a turfed backyard the same size as the house. There are three entry or exit points: the front door, the side yard gate, or hopping the backyard fence. Hopping the backyard fence is clutch because it connects directly to the Lee Arms apartments, which house mainly sorority girls.

Our squad walks to White Picket and we can hear the electronic beats coming from the backyard. The backyard has a tented dance area with a DJ and an outdoor bar to the side. The place isn't packed yet, but there's about 50 people already there. The indoor living room turned dance floor has more hip-hop-y music playing.

I say my hellos once again. This time to all the upperclassmen present. The music from the outdoor EDM DJ doesn't make me want to dance like everyone else. The music from the indoor aux is more my taste, but no one is dancing to it. My hands are empty and I'm already tired of the futile small talk. Time for a drink.

Having finished my pregame drink, I head to the raggedy wooden bar out back which is manned by two sober fraternity brothers. I notice there's a large Gatorade cooler which is dispensing the red liquid everyone is drinking. Jungle juice?

It must be a light alcoholic drink because it's being served in red Solo cups that one would use for beer pong. "Let me get some of that, bro." As if it makes a difference I also ask, "What alcohol is in it?" The bartender yells over the EDM beats, "Burnett's!"

At Cal Poly, Burnett's is notorious for being one of the cheapest, nastiest vodkas out there. I would never drink this by choice, but since there's no other option, I accept the drink.

As I turn away, I realize he only poured me about half a Solo cup of the red jungle juice. Hmm, maybe he thought I was already too drunk. I gulp it down within a few minutes. They did a great job mixing the jungle juice to mask the horrendous taste of Burnett's. Another drink down to the liver.

I bounce around the party, socializing from the kitchen to porch to living room to backyard. Once each section of the party bores me, I head to the bar to re-up my jungle juice. There's about 5 servings of jungle juices down to my liver now.

There's plenty of pretty women. The majority of them are either blonde or brunette white women. I'm the only darkskin Black man, and there are no darkskin Black women present.

One frustrating part about partying at a PWI is feeling uninvited, even though I was literally invited to party.

I've noticed the same phenomenon at every party thus far, including this one. I walk through a crowded party and am immediately noticed by everyone because of my 6'4" height—6'7" if you count my afro. People turn their heads and eyes towards me. Those who know me (mostly my fraternity brothers), are elated to see me and proceed to greet me with love and respect.

But with those who don't know me, (mostly the women invitees), it's a totally different story. After they turn their heads and eyes towards me, their gazes freeze for a moment. In the standstill, I can tell their minds are processing various thoughts.

The women are not gazing at me because it's love at first sight or because I'm a 10 out of 10. No, I'm not attractive enough to garner that kind of attention.

Instead, the women momentarily gaze at me because they either feel unsure, confused, threatened, curious, or a fetish. Their change in facial expressions and body language says it all. They wonder a range of inebriated questions.

"Who is that guy?" "Is he in Sigma Nu?" "Is he one of Cal Poly's athletes?" "Who does he know here?" "How did he get invited?" "Did he sneak into this party?" "Is he safe to interact with?" "Is he friendly?" "Is he into women like me?" "Is his dick big like they say?"

As if we can telepathically communicate, my drunk mind wonders too.

"Is she looking at me?" "Why is she looking at me?" "Is she a Trump supporter?" "Is she racist?" "Can I trust her?" "Is she comfortable with Black men?" "Does she have jungle fever?"

A drunk mind speaks a sober heart, I guess.

It's discouraging every time this happens,but I push on with grace and patience. Perhaps these women have never interacted with a tall Black man—or maybe I'm overthinking. Assumptions, assumptions.

The alcohol definitely helps to subdue this awkward tension between me and a predominantly white population of college women.

I believe Americans are notorious for overindulgence of alcohol, partly because it's liquid courage to help us confront or ignore the phobias which plague our country. These are the muses which enter my head on the daily, even when I'm intoxicated.

By now, I'm drunk drunk—to the point where I'm dancing to EDM. I try my best to find a beat to bop to, but it's literally impossible with all the drops and mixing. This is why I don't like EDM.

The DJ booth has several strobe lights flashing to the beats. There's even a fog machine, making the tented dance floor more like a movie. Smiling, jumping, with hands in the air, everyone seems to be having an amazing time.

I transition over to the bar again, but get caught up in a conversation with my pledge bro, Ben, and four beautiful ladies in their third year. One of them squeals, "let's go take another shot!" Ben and I are down, so we ask where. One of the girls points past the backyard and yells, "at our apartment!"

Ben and I look at each other with glee that we're being escorted by juniors to their apartment for shots. We follow the ladies behind the tent towards the farthest corner of the backyard.

I'm wearing my chameleon Jordan 6s, so I cautiously step through the dimly lit path of dirt, empty beer cans, and probably human feces. We arrive at the backyard's corner and scale the six-foot tall spiked fence using some conveniently placed bricks.

Once we all throw ourselves over the fence spikes, we head upstairs and into an apartment living room. On the table is a bottle of pineapple Ciroc vodka. "Let's take these shots!" one sorority sister shouts as she scurries to the kitchen for shot glasses. The others plop on the couch, run to the bathroom, or head to their bedroom.

Ben and I wait awkwardly by the Ciroc. In sync, all the women return and we take a celebratory group shot with no chaser. Ciroc is so much smoother than Burnett's, my goodness. Another shot of vodka to the liver.

Just as I thought we were going to return to the party, which is visible from this apartment, one of the ladies insists, "one more shot before we go back!"

I side-eye Ben because I don't know if I should take another shot. Before I can firmly refuse, my shot glass is full. Welp. Another shot to the liver. We wobble out and down the stairs, then sloppily scale the pointed fence once again. With no regard for my Jordans, or the guy peeing beside me, I mob myself back into the party around midnight.

I wake up in a bright room. I'm extremely groggy and it's taking time for my blurry vision to fade. To my left I see Brett, even though I don't remember partying with him. Beside him is Ted, who wasn't even at the party. On the other side is a nurse.

I try to say something and muster energy to get out of the hospital bed. Instead, I only manage to groan and lift my head. "Take it easy buddy. No rush getting up," whispers the nurse with her hand on my shoulder.

I pass out again and wake up this time with enough energy to speak. "What happened?" I mumble to Brett. "You drank too much, bud. When you're ready, let's get out of here and I'll tell you the rest."

I look over to the nurse, "okay, I'm ready to go." She comfortably replies, "alright sweetie, let me show you to the front desk for the hospital bill, then you can go home."

"The hospital bill?!" I whisper-shout with the little energy left in my still-drunk body. Everybody except me laughs at my honest and naive idealism. A drunk mind speaks a sober tongue, I guess.

Bruh, why isn't health care free? The sun hasn't even risen yet and they didn't perform an operation. How could this cost money?

I'm wheelchaired out into the hallway, where the front desk hands me a folded hospital bill. I open it as we walk out the building and into the dawn. $1500!?!?

There's no way. This has to be a joke. I was in there for no more than 4 hours. Ridiculous. Brett insists I worry about it later and rest in his apartment. Still drunk, I pass out on Brett's couch around 7AM.

—

I almost died that night. How close I was to death, I'll never really know. I blacked out around midnight, so whatever happened after that I had to piece together from those who were at the party.

Apparently no one realized I was blacked out. I was behaving quite normally for my standards. Quite scary that I control my outward appearance so tightly to the point where people can't immediately tell if I'm intoxicated.

They say that around 2AM, I passed out on the couch near the kitchen. Some came to check on me, but I wouldn't wake up, speak, or even open my eyes. They tried slapping me in the face six times, and the only response my body gave was a faint groan.

One of the brothers sent an SOS to the fraternity groupchat, requesting a sober driver to White Picket ASAP. As fate would have it, only one person, Ted, responded to that 2AM message. Ted, who was asleep in his own bed, told me he only saw the message because he got up to pee. As soon as he saw it, he rushed to White Picket, where it took several strong fraternity men to carry my limp 170-pound body into his truck. Riding in Ted's truck saved me about $3000 in ambulance fees.

Regarding my $1500 hospital bill, I had two options: pay the bill upfront in cash with my own money, or use my family's health insurance so I only pay a $50 co-pay fee. I elected to use my family's insurance. This meant I could not hide from this shameful night, since it would appear on our insurance statements. This was the right decision, despite the uncomfortable phone calls I made to both my parents.

After some reflection, I realized I made one especially fatal error that night. I failed to determine how much alcohol was in the jungle juice. I figured since it was a juice, its alcohol content would be similar to that of a cocktail or strong beer.

Later, I learned the alcohol content of the jungle juice was more like a straight shot of hard liquor.

I was fooled by the size of the solo cups. After all, people typically drink shots in shot glasses, and mixed drinks in cups—not the other way around.

Well, I guess it's now evident that my academic struggles during the spring quarter of my freshman year were in part due to my social behavior.

Thank God for my community that night, because they likely saved my life. And I do not say that lightly, because in 2008, Carson Starkey, a Cal Poly student was left for dead on a mattress after a former fraternity's initiation event [21].

No matter how strong your individual faith or mentality is, we all need community—a good and loyal community. Because your community will be the earthly ones who show up for you, when you can't look out for yourself.

Besides protecting you, an ironclad community can sharpen you. If you are lacking in anything, the right community can enhance your academics, mentality, faith, and more—just as iron sharpens iron.

So thus far, the three foundational layers that literally carried me through college are faith, mentality, and community. It is my belief that if you have a solid foundation of faith (Chapter 4), a healthy mentality (Chapter 5), and a supportive community (Chapter 6, 7), you will withstand any collegiate calamity which comes your way.

By the way, I'm not here to tell you what you should or shouldn't do regarding alcohol, drugs, or anything really. It is not my place, because I have my own self to work on first.

What I *am* telling you is, based on my experience, the fire is HOT and it *will* burn you to ashes if you choose to touch it! While its warmth may provide relief, if you play with fire, the consequences are yours to bear! For yourself, discern what is fire and what isn't. How close to the flames is too close? How much heat can you handle before you collapse?

Minus academics, your first year is perhaps the hardest to overcome of all years of college. Faith, mentality, and community are three nearly intangible aspects to build on. But the good news is after that first year, everything (except academics) should get easier, assuming you built a solid personal foundation.

And the even better news is the foundation you construct for yourself in college can stay with you for the rest of your life. If you haven't noticed already, college is nothing more than preparation for life after college.

Welcome to adult life and the "real" world, my friend :)

Part III

SOPHOMORE
(Preview)

Though the slogan on America's silver coins says "In God We Trust", we deny this as we set out to collect as many of these coins as we can.

Uell S. Andersen, "Three Magic Words" (1954)

8

Closed Mouths Don't Get Bread (Preview)

What good is a solid community if you don't communicate when you need resources to help you out? The right resources in college can get you scholarship money, mentors, and even things like prime housing. I'll explain...

Since I prefer to let the money talk, let me just start by transparently sharing how my bachelor's and master's education ($125,000) was funded with the help of grants and scholarships. Hopefully you notice a theme.

8.1 Grants + Scholarships (Budget)

Table 8.1: A full list of grants I was awarded and when they were awarded during my five years at Cal Poly.

List of Grants		
Grant Program	**Amount**	**Year**
Cal Grant A	$5,472	1st
Cal Grant A	$5,472	2nd
Cal Grant A	$5,472	3rd
Cal Grant A	$5,472	4th
COVID-19 C.A.R.E.S. Act Grant	$550	4th
Cal Poly Cares Emergency Grant	$550	4th
COVID-19 Cal Poly NSBE Grant	$200	4th
COVID-19 Cal Poly Summer Grant	$1,800	5th
California State University Grant	$7,176	5th
Health Services Fee Grant	$435	5th
Federal HEERF II Act Grant	$1,350	5th
COVID-19 Cal Poly NSBE Grant 2.0	$200	5th
Total: $34,149		

Table 8.2: A full list of my scholarship sources and when they were awarded during my five years at Cal Poly.

List of Scholarships		
Scholarship Source	**Amount**	**Year**
William J. Coffey Memorial	$1,500	1st
Alpha Kappa Alpha Sorority	$500	1st
Conejo Youth Basketball Association	$500	1st
Delta Sigma Theta Sorority	$500	1st
Kiwanis Club of Thousand Oaks, Mel Ashcraft Scholarship	$1,000	1st
Unknown (I can't find the name lol)	$2,000	1st
The Links	$500	1st
Omega Psi Phi Fraternity	$500	1st
Sigma Nu - Kappa Pi Chapter	$100	1st
African American Male Education Network & Development (A2MEND)	$1,500	1st
Cal Poly, National Society of Black Engineers (NSBE), GPA Improvement	$25	1st
Cal Poly, Multicultural Engineering Program (MEP), Leadership to Legacy	$500	2nd
A2MEND	$1,500	2nd
Sigma Nu - Kappa Pi Chapter	$100	2nd
Cal Poly, MEP, Leadership to Legacy	$600	3rd
A2MEND	$1,500	3rd
NSBE, Board of Corporate Affiliates	$2,500	3rd
Cal Poly, Louis Stokes Alliance for Minority Participation (LSAMP)	$1,250	4th
A2MEND	$1,000	4th
Cal Poly, MEP / Chevron	$2,000	5th
California Community Foundation	$3,000	5th
NSBE, NV5 Global Inc.	$5,000	5th
NSBE, Board of Corporate Affiliates	$2,000	5th
Total: $29,575		

Behind every one of these line items is a story of how I received the money. And every single story involves me sticking my neck out into my network and intentionally seeking support...

TO BE CONTINUED...

9
Author's Notes

Fall 2022

Hi,

Thanks for reading this far into my book. I hope it's helpful in some way. I'm still writing about my remaining years of college so I would appreciate your patience and encouragement. Releasing the initial publication of this series is really me just testing the waters. I would love to hear your feedback, whether positive or negative! It will help and motivate me to write my subsequent publications better... or to stop writing if it's that bad lol.

If the ending to this book left you wanting more, then good, because I have much more to share! God willing, future publications in this series will cover a **range** of my experiences in college. I plan for the second publication to chronicle my sophomore and junior years. In my sophomore year I added three more important layers to my personal foundation: resourcefulness, volunteerism, and leadership. In my junior year I added internships, productivity, and traveling. Then, I hope for the third and final publication to chronicle my senior and graduate years at Cal Poly. In my senior year I added study abroad, diet, and protesting to my personal foundation. In my graduate year I added local politics, genocide, and relationships.

I have relatable experiences and vivid memories for each of these foundational layers. Hopefully my life stories serve as a resource for today's generation of students and as a time capsule for scholars in the generations to come.

I'm pleased to inform you that this book you are reading is entirely self-published and unrelated to my full-time day job. Meaning, no one paid or pressured me to write this and I funded the production and printing of this product through the management of my limited liability company, AMMAN LLC, under the imprint, Gen Z(eal) Publications.

Pray for me!
Amman

9.1 Acknowledgments

My sincere gratitude and appreciation goes to the many folks for helping make this publication a reality. First, Katherine for meeting with me weekly to do progress checks when the book was at its infancy. Next, my former college roommates, Aidan and DJ, for helping create a psychologically safe home and cheering me on as the book began to develop. And last but not least, my beta readers, Samhal, Mahelet, Edin, Matthew, and Gideon for being the first ones to read the entire book and help me iterate it to the finish line.

10
Bibliography

References

[1] *Fall 2016 PolyView: Characteristics of Students Enrolled at Cal Poly, San Luis Obispo*. English. 2016. URL: https://content-calpoly-edu.s3.amazonaws.com/ir/1/images/Fall%202016%20PolyView_3.pdf.

[2] *Fall 2021 PolyView: Characteristics of Students Enrolled at Cal Poly, San Luis Obispo*. English. 2016. URL: https://content-calpoly-edu.s3.amazonaws.com/ir/1/images/POLYVIEW_2021%20Combined_5.PDF.

[3] "Cal Poly is the whitest public university in California — by a lot". In: *San Luis Obispo Tribune Newspaper* (Apr. 2018). URL: https://www.google.com/url?sa=t&rct=j&q=&esrc=s&source=web&cd=&cad=rja&uact=8&ved=2ahUKEwiG_tG5u477AhWHHTQIHQOFAIIQFnoECAsQAQ&url=

https%3A%2F%2Fwww.sanluisobispo.com%2Fnews%2Flocal%2Feducation%2Farticle209195019.html&usg=AOvVaw2_LHQqz8lEQZILlopVfTYK.

[4] *QuickFacts California*. July 2021. URL: https://www.census.gov/quickfacts/CA.

[5] Megan Schellong. "The blackface scandal that rocked my campus". English. In: *BBC News* (Nov. 2018). URL: https://www.bbc.com/news/stories-46322875.

[6] Ashley Ladin. "Sigma Nu Becomes First Cal Poly Greek Chapter To Create A Diversity Chair Position". English. In: *Mustang News* (May 2018). URL: https://mustangnews.net/sigma-nu-becomes-first-cal-poly-greek-chapter-to-create-a-diversity-chair-position/.

[7] Amman Fasil Asfaw. *Food4Thought*. Music Playlist. San Luis Obispo, CA, Dec. 2018. URL: http://bit.ly/Food4ThoughtSpotify.

[8] Maya Angelou. *I Know Why the Caged Bird Sings*. English. Random House Publishing Group, 1969.

[9] Maya Angelou. *Caged Bird*. English. Poem. 1983. URL: https://www.poetryfoundation.org/poems/48989/caged-bird.

[10] Paul Laurence Dunbar. *Sympathy*. English. Poem. 1899. URL: https://www.poetryfoundation.org/poems/46459/sympathy-56d22658afbc0.

[11] Various. "Lessons Learned". English. In: *Cal Poly Magazine* (Jan. 2019). URL: https://magazine.calpoly.edu/year-in-review-2018/lessons-learned-2018/.

[12] *Habesha peoples*. en. Page Version ID: 1093746249. June 2022. URL: https://en.wikipedia.org/w/index.php?title=Habesha_peoples&oldid=1093746249 (visited on 06/22/2022).

[13] *Red Terror (Ethiopia)*. en. Page Version ID: 1092619073. June 2022. URL: https://en.wikipedia.org/w/index.php?title=Red_Terror_(Ethiopia)&oldid=1092619073 (visited on 06/22/2022).

[14] Tadesse Beyene Wereta. "Ethnobotany of medicinal plants in Erob and Gulomahda districts, Eastern Zone of Tigray Region, Ethiopia". en. In: (), p. 338. URL: http://213.55.95.56/bitstream/handle/123456789/9335/Tadesse%20Beyene.pdf?sequence=1&isAllowed=y.

[15] *Eritrean War of Independence (Eritrean Revolution)*. en. Page Version ID: 10841-34898. Apr. 2022. URL: https://en.wikipedia.org/w/index.php?title=Eritrean_War_of_Independence&oldid=1084134898 (visited on 06/22/2022).

[16] *Eritrean–Ethiopian War*. en. Page Version ID: 1092126197. June 2022. URL: https://en.wikipedia.org/w/index.php?title=Eritrean%E2%80%93Ethiopian_War&oldid=1092126197 (visited on 06/22/2022).

[17] *Famines in Ethiopia*. en. Page Version ID: 1090100366. May 2022. URL: https://en.wikipedia.org/w/index.php?title=Famines_in_Ethiopia&oldid=1090100366 (visited on 06/22/2022).

[18] *Sunken eyes: Causes, pictures, and how to get rid of them*. en. Nov. 2017. URL: https://www.medicalnewstoday.com/articles/320134 (visited on 06/22/2022).

[19] Max Rosenberg Guey Lynne. *Thirteen Schools Where It's Almost Impossible To Fail*. en-US. URL: https://www.businessinsider.com/13-schools-where-its-really-hard-to-fail-2013-5 (visited on 06/22/2022).

[20] *Mardi Gras*. en. Page Version ID: 1091517557. June 2022. URL: https://en.wikipedia.org/w/index.php?title=Mardi_Gras&oldid=1091517557 (visited on 06/22/2022).

[21] *Carson's Story — Aware Awake Alive.* URL: https://awareawakealive.org/about/carsons-story (visited on 06/22/2022).